Entertaining with Magimix

Nicola Cox

ictc

First published 1984 by the Publishing Division of ICTC Ltd.,
632-652 London Road, Isleworth, Middlesex, TW13 4EZ

British Library Cataloguing in Publication Data

Cox, Nicola
    Entertaining with Magimix
      1. Entertaining   2. Food processor cookery
      I. Title
      641.5'68   TX731

ISBN 0 907642 10 1

Designed and photographed by Edward Piper
Edited by Tessa Hayward

Printed in Great Britain by Chorley & Pickersgill Ltd, Leeds

ICTC Stock Number: 54130

The author and publisher would like to thank Divertimenti,
68-72 Marylebone Lane, London W1M 5FF for the loan of the
accessories used in the photographs on pages 44, 49

The dishes and china on pages 18, 27, 95, 99, 113 are from ICTC Ltd.

The French Country Range shown on page 6 is by courtesy of
Marks and Spencer p.l.c.

The photograph on the back of the book and on page 106 was taken
by kind permission of Stowe School

Contents

Introduction

———————⟨ ✦ ⟩———————

Cooking and sharing food with others has always been one of life's greatest pleasures and in Britain we have evolved a modern approach to entertaining which is, I think, the envy of the world. I am thrilled to have this chance to write a book on entertaining because I love it and because it gives me a marvellous opportunity to develop my ideas of this modern approach together with the Magimix, surely the greatest new aid to cooking since the stove was invented and we ceased cooking on an open fire.

Ever since lords kept great houses and entertained lavishly, hospitality has been our tradition. At the end of the second world war, however, hostesses and housewives were faced with immense problems; food was scarce, interesting imported ingredients difficult to find, money for food was short and those previously lucky enough to have staff found themselves left to cope on their own. But these intelligent young women, undaunted and put on their mettle by a war, were not going to allow these small deprivations to stand in the way of their entertaining. Into the kitchen they went, learning to cook for themselves and, not having been taught at mother's knee, they had a questioning approach as to the best, quickest and easiest way to do things.

Gradually cookery schools grew up to help them, and then their daughters, so now a genuine interest in good food and cooking has been established. On the continent, home entertaining still tends to mean formal and rather grand occasions, perhaps ordering the food from caterers or getting someone in to do it, or even more frequently entertaining in restaurants. Go into any private house in France, and you will be invited to enjoy course after traditional course – delicious but not conducive to frequent entertaining – while in Britain we have adapted to a more modern style altogether with good but less pretentious food. I

also think we are more imaginative in our choice of dishes; we may serve Caribbean Chicken or Peking Duck while the French will still stick to their tradition of Coq au Vin or Cassoulet and the Germans play waltz tunes on the ubiquitous Weiner Schnitzels.

We serve things simply, often with style and flair, but probably eat in the kitchen (now so often the most lived-in room of the house). Both freezer and Magimix are thoroughly utilised to take the brunt of the work so that the kitchen no longer holds the whip hand. Although our lives seem to get more hectic and hurried, we do undoubtedly have more leisure time; how better to spend some of it than in cooking and entertaining – for isn't sitting round a table, eating and drinking with friends, one of the pleasantest forms of relaxation imaginable? Restaurants are expensive, and can be disappointing, so the answer must be home entertaining, using all the help and modern aids as well as the simpler modern styles of cooking, but definitely rejecting the 'mix two cans and sprinkle with a packet' approach.

The first course might be a smooth soup, pâté or mousse, all dishes that until recently were frequently rejected because of the hard work involved. Sieving soups, pounding pâtés and puréeing mousses were just what the post war cook found so difficult to find time for, but now with Magimix, they are some of the easiest and best starters imaginable. Incidentally, soups, mousses, pâtés and pies are some of the dishes that foreigners most admire in British cooking.

Main courses can now be anything, come from anywhere, and there is no need to worry about the old, formal convention of soup, entrée and roast. The simple and superlative British roast is still enjoyed as much as ever, but so are new flavours, tastes and textures, all of which offer the creative cook excitement and pleasure to prepare.

Nowadays, some people have cheese instead of pudding. I love cheese and I often serve it because it's quick and easy to prepare. But don't forget it's also difficult to find at its best and you may take just as long, or longer, ferreting it out from your nearest market. Some men pretend they don't like puddings but don't be taken in by that: serve them and you will find most men will enjoy your finest creations. While I may serve cheese as well, puddings for me have always been a chance to create something special, to enjoy myself as a cook and leave me with the sweet taste of success at the end of the meal; now, with my Magimix to help, I'm certainly not going to do without them.

Cooking and entertaining with a Magimix is easy and unconfined because you have the equivalent of at least another pair of hands in the kitchen. With the freezer to act as one of your storerooms and your uninhibited modern lack of convention, you may do as you please – but please enjoy what you do! If you want to have only a starter and a main course, do so without apologising because that's usually all one has in a restaurant. These days it really is up to you.

The excitement, for me, is that here is a simple book, definitely outside the glossy coffee table range, that really is for use in the kitchen. It's a book in which I have suggested ideas for different types of entertaining from dinner parties through picnics to childrens' parties. Indeed, it's food for all sorts of occasions which, at some stage, could apply to us all.

I have taken the opportunity to expand on certain points, rather as I do in my demonstrations, for example to talk about menu planning or boiling caramel, as well as trying to give all the little hints and tips one discovers in making a dish many times over and which I hope will save you having to discover them for yourself. I try to suggest lots of alternatives and with a really good index you can of course mix and match as you will, taking something from here and something from there to give your entertaining your own signature.

It is intended to be a book to encourage cooking and entertaining. I know from my wide experience of demonstrating how much is learned by looking; you only have to see a dish cooked and you know without a word being said how it should be, the thickness of the sliced onions, the size of the meat cubes, the consistency of the sauce or the texture of the dough. All these are so difficult to put into words – how thick is thick, how fine is fine – so we've got lots of pictures to make it as visual as possible.

So join me and entertain in these different ways. With a family of four children, all these parties have happened in our house and everything has been tried on critical guinea pigs of one age or another. I hope that you enjoy your entertaining with Magimix!

Acknowledgements

I don't know what I would have done without Simon. Saint that he is, he not only tastes and criticizes recipe after recipe with only occasionally flagging enthusiasm, but is then prepared to discuss, correct, edit and proof read them to try to achieve perfect recipes. I would also like to thank my girls for all the months of testing and trying, weighing and adjusting to make sure each recipe is well and truly tested and really works, and for their help during a hectic fortnight of photography. My grateful thanks are also due to our secretary, Mrs James, who typed her little fingers to the bone to make sure we got the manuscript finished on time.

Very many thanks to Tessa Hayward, for her careful editing and willingness and ability to interpret our ideas and to Edward Piper whose knowledge, expertise and infallible eye for photography and book layout has been a great contribution.

My thanks also to Julian Cotterell for asking me to do it in the first place and for giving us the fun of trying out all these different parties. We've enjoyed doing it.

Nicola Cox

MENU	*Variations*
Chicken Liver Pâté served with Crusty Bread or Hot Toast	**Chicken Liver Tartlettes.** This is a hot alternative, more time-consuming to make but very good.
	Chicken Liver Terrine. The same filling but served cold from a terrine.
——	
Spiced Chicken with Tomato and Cheese	**Sauté of Chicken with Creamy Tomato Sauce.** A delicate and more elegant alternative to the Spiced Chicken.
Gratin of Potato	
Braised Peas with Bacon and Onion	**Petits Pois à la Français.** A classic dish, and a good match for the Sauté of Chicken; or use simply cooked courgettes or any other vegetable in season.
——	
Banana and Ginger Praliné	**Banana, Guava and Rum Praliné.** An alternative for those who don't like ginger.
	Yoghurt and Cream Topped Fruit Praliné. The use of yoghurt instead of cream and some lime or lemon provides a less rich alternative.
	Almond Shortbread Fingers. These add that little extra crunch and endorse the almond note.

The Reliable Dinner or Supper Party

—◆—

We all need reliable friends who never let us down, who are always available, who turn up trumps whenever we need them and fit into all occasions. Well, this menu is just that. It is reliable and it's made from ingredients that are nearly always around. It's quick and easy to prepare and can be dressed up or down to suit your purse, your mood and the time you have available for cooking. I love to have one or two menus like this up my sleeve because they give me a nice safe feeling, especially when no other brilliant inspiration strikes me and I have bludgeoned my brains to no avail. I know I can fall back on it, confident that I can trust it and that I can vary it in many ways to fit the bill.

Menu planning is a great art that is learnt gradually, and is often the most difficult part of preparing for a party, though in many ways the most interesting. The Chinese are masters of this art with their beautifully subtle dishes that display different colours, tastes and textures. I believe we can acquire this knowledge reasonably quickly if we follow three basic rules (which we must be quite prepared to break when we want to) and are prepared to give a little thought to applying them. I keep these main headings in my mind as I build my menu and use it as a check list once I have completed it.

Season. Shall I consciously choose a seasonal dish, like game, asparagus or strawberries, that is at its best? Or will what I wish to use, like watercress for the soup, be available in August? Or do I want to have something that is traditional with, say, the Easter season like a plump capon or some baby lamb? I probably subconsciously rule out dishes that I think unseasonal and don't often have, for instance, a steamed pudding in June.

Balance. Have I got fish or chicken in two courses (I may choose to, but on purpose, not inadvertently)? Have I used cream in every course, and is my meal too rich – or is it plain and dull? Does my menu build course on course towards a climax because dish should ideally lead into dish and wine to wine? Are there any little touches like cheese straws with the first course or pastry fingers with the pudding which will just tip the scales and complete the balance and harmony?

Contrast. Will the dishes complement each other with the right contrasts of texture, colour, flavour and style?

As a start, I think of one of the dishes I wish to serve. This will usually be the main course, but it can just as easily be a first course or pudding. I may choose it because it is particularly in season, because my guests will especially enjoy it, or just because I have it available. Maybe I want to try something new or cook something that is quick and easy to prepare when I know I have not got much time. Whatever the reason, it gives me a beginning from which I can build, always keeping S.B.C. (season, balance and contrast) in mind. Maybe I will jump to another course without completing the accompaniments to my first idea, for what goes with it may vary depending on the content, richness or colour of another course. Gradually my main ideas, accompanying themes and the final little touches will come together to make a complete meal.

For everyday meals, this process is computerised in the experienced mind with the nutritional value of the meal also being taken into account automatically and the whole process taking only a few seconds. 'We will have tomato soup, fish fingers, mashed potatoes and peas with baked apples and rice pudding to follow'. All the rules of season, balance and contrast have been taken into account but almost subconsciously. For a party or special menu, we only have to do the same thing but taking rather more care and trouble, but that is really all there is to it.

Let's look at this menu, see why we chose it and how it can be varied by being dressed up or down. Our basic menu is a simple, quickly made chicken liver pâté which can be served with fresh bread or toast, followed by a robust, rustic and tasty sauté of chicken with tomatoes and cheese. Some would say you could not follow chicken liver pâté with a chicken dish but that would be nonsense for the flavour, texture and content of the pâté is totally different to portions of chicken and therefore does not give you an unbalanced menu. A green vegetable looks good, so we use a delicious but simply made and reheated dish of frozen petit pois. An unobtrusive gratin of potatoes won't detract from the sauté of chicken and the potatoes are very quickly and easily sliced with the Magimix. We follow with bananas (available all year) and stem ginger in syrup (off the store cupboard shelf), always a felicitous combination, topped with whipped cream (we have used no cream in the menu so far) and powdered caramel-nut praline, delicious and easy to make in the Magimix.

That's our basic menu, always available but also easy, quick and robustly tasty. Now let's play tunes upon it. We can make our pâté more delicate but richer by adding eggs and cream to it; or we can cook the enriched cream version in little cream cheese pastry tartlettes and serve them hot; or we can cook it in a terrine and serve it cold. We can season and spice the main course chicken more delicately and serve it in a smooth and delicate cream and tomato sauce, lifting it from the rustic and robust to the world of simple haute cuisine; Puff Pastry Shapes (or heart shaped croutes of fried bread if you served tartlettes to start with) and classic Petits Pois à la Français or delicate baby courgettes, perfectly cooked, will also raise the tone of the dish and give it a more sophisticated touch. The gratin could stay unchanged, for it is intended to be unobtrusive, but the pudding might now prove a little rich as we are using cream in the first two courses. So maybe we will fold plain yoghurt into our whipped cream to lighten it and add a touch of acidity with a squeeze of lime over the bananas and a little grated lime rind with the praline. Or perhaps we prefer a lighter fruit pudding altogether and turn to Pineapple and Banana in Caramel Syrup, spiked with a grain or two of cardamom (a variation of the recipe on page 31). Almond Shortbread Fingers can be added to enhance any of these pudding variations, depending on what you have used for the first or main course.

So with a little more time, trouble and effort, but retaining our simple and available basic ingredients, we can shift this menu from tasty and robust to delicate and fine, making it suitable for either summer or winter but always choosing a version that is just right for our chosen occasion. This is the art of menu planning.

Shopping and Preparation

The basic menu has kept shopping and unusual ingredients to a minimum for, if you are in a hurry, complicated shopping and poring over recipes to make sure nothing is forgotten can take as much time as the cooking. In fact, it is so often the planning and organisation which takes the time, so for this basic menu I am including a combined ingredient list, divided into various types just as I would at home; this allows you to see at a glance what you need from the shops or your store cupboard. I can't do this for all the variations; it would get too complicated but having chosen your preferred menu and variations, you can quickly do the same and have a fingertip check-list of what you need.

The shopping can take place a day or so ahead, though the chicken livers (all the better for being made into pâté several days ahead) will make the best tartlettes when really fresh. Of course, this basic menu expects that you may want to use the freezer, and the chicken livers, chicken and peas can all come out of the freezer (that's partly what makes it so useful), but for the refined and dressed up versions, always remember that the better and fresher your ingredients, the better the dish.

Cooking Countdown for Basic Menu

2–3 Days Ahead
Make chicken liver pâté and keep it in a fridge or larder (though of course you can make it shortly before eating it if you wish).
Make praline powder (which stores quite well for this length of time) though is perhaps better when fresh.

1 Day Ahead
Joint and season chicken (if you wish and you are starting with a whole chicken).
Prepare braised peas.

The Day
Make pâté, or remove from fridge half a day ahead to serve at room temperature.
Make praline if not already made.
Prepare banana and ginger praliné.
Prepare and cook gratin at least *1½ hours ahead*; it must be cooked once prepared but will keep warm obligingly.
Sauté and cook chicken at least *1 hour ahead*; keep warm ready to top with cheese and grill.

Last Minute
Make toast or heat bread if necessary.
Top chicken with cheese and flash under grill.
Top bananas with praline.

Basic Menu Ingredients List

Meat and Fish	Fruit and Veg	Dairy	Herbs and Spices	Etc
8 oz chicken livers	5–6 onions: (1 onion +8 oz+1 onion)	12 oz butter: (6+ 2½+½+3 oz)	quatre épice or ground allspice	1 tablespoon brandy
6–8 portions chicken	1 lb tomatoes	18 fl oz whipping cream (3+5+ 10 fl oz)	parsley	olive oil
4 oz thick sliced smoked bacon	3½ lb potatoes		fresh or dried basil	1 tin beef consommé
	2 lb peas	8 oz mild cheddar or mozzarella cheese	bayleaf	sugar
	1 lettuce (or outside leaves)	½ pt milk	fresh or dried marjoram	¼ chicken stock cube
	8 ripe bananas	2 eggs	garlic	ginger in syrup
			fresh fennel or fennel seed	2 oz whole or flaked almonds
			black peppercorns	2 oz whole hazelnuts
			sea salt	
			nutmeg	

Chicken Liver Pâté

Taking only moments to make, this simple but nevertheless delicious pâté is a tried and true friend. Nothing original here, I know, for probably chicken liver pâté is one of the most frequently made, or even overmade, dishes to hit us since food processors came on the market and pressing pâtés through a hair sieve went out of fashion. But well made and carefully flavoured, it is still thoroughly enjoyed and is a wonderful relief from those ghastly pet-food pâtés sold in some supermarkets.

Chicken livers are funny things. They have a very strong flavour which is vastly improved by careful dilution with some blander substance. I have found that if I use a high proportion of butter, much higher than is used in most recipes, the pâté has a creamy texture and a strong but not overpowering flavour that appeals to far more people than the conventional dark brown, crumbly mixture. If you dilute them still further, as in the tartlettes or in the baked terrine

variation, you will find the flavour truer and finer.

Chicken livers must be firm and fresh, the lighter in colour the better because pale livers come from well fattened birds. They should remain firm when you cook them; if they crumble in the pan, it is a sure indication of staleness or poor freezing (they freeze perfectly well and should come out just as firm and fresh as they went in, though limit their freezer life to about six months).

Chicken livers need careful checking to make sure they are not tainted with bile, the bitter green substance that lies in a little bag just beside the liver. Should there be any green-tinged flesh on the liver, remove it, for even the faintest suspicion of bile can ruin the whole dish, giving it an unattractive bitter flavour. The little tubes and threads which connect each half of the liver also need to be carefully removed to ensure a smooth mixture. Domestic duck livers, turkey livers and even guinea-fowl livers could all be used for these dishes but I am always a little suspicious of pheasant or game bird livers

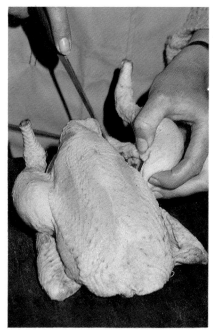

To joint a chicken use a sharp knife and start by cutting off both the legs where they meet the carcase

Continue by using a pair of strong scissors and detaching the bottom half of the carcase by cutting diagonally from the tip of the breastbone to the neck underneath the breast and then the wing. Keep the carcase for making a stock

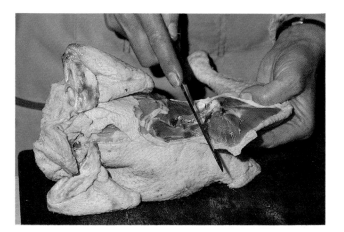

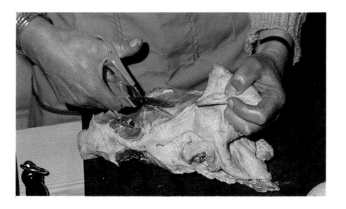

because the long hanging time tends to allow the bile to permeate the livers.

for 6–8 people
8 oz (225 g) chicken livers
1 small onion
4–6 oz (100–175 g) butter
¼ teaspoon quatre épice or ground allspice
1 tablespoon finely chopped parsley
a little fresh or pinch dried marjoram
1 tablespoon brandy
salt and pepper

Use the double-bladed knife. Roughly chop the onion using the on/off technique and soften gently in half the butter in a frying pan. Pick over the livers, carefully removing any threads and green-tinged flesh which will give them a bitter taste. Cut each liver into 2–3 pieces. Once the onion is softened, turn up the heat, add the livers and sauté briskly until sealed; then add quatre épice or allspice and seasoning;

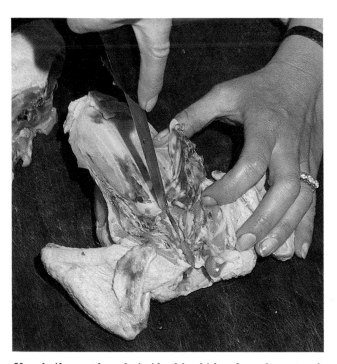

Use a knife to cut from the inside of the chicken down the centre of the breast and then remove the end joints of the legs and the wing tips

If you wish to have eight joints you can cut the wing from the breast and halve the legs at the middle joint

cover and continue to cook, but over a very low heat until the chicken livers are just cooked but still rosy inside.

Turn them into the Magimix bowl, still with the double-bladed knife in place, add the herbs and process until quite smooth; then cut the remaining butter into little pieces and drop it in through the feed tube. Process until amalgamated and finally add the brandy. Correct the seasoning, pack into a serving dish and leave to firm up. To make a lighter and softer pâté, you could fold a few tablespoons of lightly whipped cream into the cooling pâté.

For maximum flavour and best spreading consistency serve at room temperature, not firm from the fridge.

—————— : ——————

Spiced Chicken with Tomato and Cheese

A spiced seasoning salt mixture, rubbed into the chicken portions, gives them plenty of flavour even before they are cooked with the tomato and basil and topped with a cheese gratin. You can, if you like, leave off the cheese as they are good without it.

for 6–8 people
6–8 portions of chicken (legs do quite well for this)
2 tablespoons olive oil
½ oz (12 g) butter
1 lb (450 g) peeled, seeded and roughly chopped
  tomatoes
3–4 leaves fresh or ¼ teaspoon dried basil
1 bay leaf
8–12 oz (225–350 g) mild cheddar or mozzarella
  cheese

Seasoning salt
1½ teaspoons fine sea salt (ordinary salt is stronger
  so adjust)
¼ teaspoon black peppercorns
1 clove garlic
6–8 leaves fresh or ½ teaspoon dried basil
pinch of fennel seeds or 1 teaspoon chopped fresh
  fennel leaves

You can use bought chicken legs or joints or start with a whole chicken and follow the photographs.

Pound up the peppercorns in a mortar then add the salt, garlic, basil and fennel and pound all to a seasoning salt; rub well into the chicken portions and leave for ½–12 hours. Heat the oil and butter in a sauté pan and fry the chicken fairly gently, for about 10 minutes on each side, until a good brown. Remove from the pan and drain off all but 2 tablespoons of the fat; return the chicken, add the tomatoes, basil and bay leaf, cover and cook gently for 20–25 minutes until chicken is just cooked. Keep warm until ready to serve.

Use fine grating or coleslaw disc. Grate the cheese. If you are using cheddar cheese, use the fine grater; mozzarella, being so soft, grates better using the coleslaw disc.

To serve. Remove the chicken portions to a shallow gratin dish where they can lie in one layer; check the seasoning and pour round the sauce. Sprinkle the cheese generously over each portion of chicken and flash under a hot grill for 3–5 minutes until just melted. Do not grill for too long, or the cheese will toughen, nor try to keep the dish warm for the cheese will go stringy. It must be served straight from the grill.

Gratin of Potato

Slice upon perfect slice, the Magimix zips through potato after potato, allowing us to make superb layered potato dishes to bake in the oven. These dishes are wonderful to accompany roast meats or made-up dishes and are very good for entertaining because they can be prepared and cooked and then kept warm or re-heated very successfully. This version, made with onions, consommé, milk, cream and eggs is bland-flavoured and not too rich which allows it to accompany a variety of dishes without intruding. The eggs in it set to a custard so the juices do not run round your plate, getting mixed up with other sauces or flavours. It is in fact a real banker that can go with practically anything.

for 6–8 people
3–3½ lb (1.35–1.6 kg) potatoes
3 oz (75 g) butter
8 oz (225 g) onions
1 clove garlic
10 fl oz (300 ml) tin Campbell's beef consommé (or good strong stock)

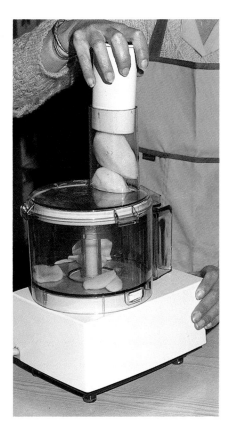

The potatoes are sliced for the Gratin which has a sauce of milk, cream and consommé

10 fl oz (300 ml) mixed milk and cream in whatever
  proportion seems suitable for your menu (usually
  I use half and half)
2 eggs
salt, pepper and freshly grated nutmeg

Use the standard slicing disc. Slice the onions and fry in half the butter in a frying pan; cook to a good brown whilst preparing everything else.

Cut the garlic clove in half and rub the cut surface of it vigorously over the base and sides of a large gratin dish; then place the two halves, lightly crushed, in a saucepan with the consommé and milk-cream mixture. Heat until nearly boiling; cover and leave to infuse. Break the eggs into a bowl, whisk with a fork, and strain on the consommé mixture. Generously butter the garlicky gratin dish, especially around the top where the potato can bake on, stick, and make the washing-up difficult. Now peel and briefly wash the potatoes but do not leave them standing in water for their natural potato starch is needed to thicken the liquid and stop the eggs from curdling.

Slice the potatoes, using moderate pressure, but don't do too many at a time, for they can go pink and discoloured very quickly. Place an overlapping layer of potatoes in the dish, season with salt, pepper and grated nutmeg, scatter over some browned onions (if they are not too hot, pick them up in your fingers and literally throw them onto the potatoes so they are evenly spread!) and pour over some of the consommé mixture. Continue with the layers, finally dot the top with the remaining butter and set the dish in a bain marie (a roasting pan with boiling water coming half way up the outside of the gratin dish). Bake in a moderately hot oven (375°F/190°C/Gas 5) for about an hour until it is completely tender when pierced with a knife and a good brown on top. Keep warm until required (this always seems better for sitting for a while) or make ahead and re-heat if you wish (one of the best gratins we ever had had been made two days ahead and re-heated) but in this case allow a little more milk so that it does not dry out.

Braised Peas with Bacon and Onion

Peas braised slowly until soft and tender acquire a quite different flavour and character to the ordinary cooked pea. They will also keep warm very happily, which is an added bonus for the cook hostess. This is loosely based on Petits Pois à la Française, but with more bacon and onion and using ordinary peas, it has a more robust flavour and is therefore more suitable for this menu. The Magimix can't really help us as this dish is so quick to do anyway.

for 6–8 people
2 lb (900 g) shelled or frozen peas
2½ oz (60 g) butter
1 large diced onion
4 oz (100 g) thick sliced smoked bacon
8–10 outside lettuce leaves if available
1 tablespoon sugar
4 or 8 tablespoons chicken stock or water and
  ¼ chicken stock cube depending on whether fresh
  or frozen peas are used (see recipe)
salt and pepper

Melt the butter in a heavy casserole, dice the bacon, add it together with the onion and fry gently until the bacon renders its fat and the onion softens but doesn't brown. Shred and add the lettuce leaves, then the peas (if frozen try not to include too much ice), sugar, stock (the larger quantity for fresh peas) and season; cover closely and cook very gently on top of the stove or in a very moderate oven (325°F/170°C/Gas 3) for 40–50 minutes (or slightly longer for frozen peas) or until the peas are very soft and tender and a little syrupy sauce is left. Add more water if it all evaporates or boil fast with the lid off if too much remains. Keep warm until required or reheat if you prefer.

Banana and Ginger Praliné

Simple, readily available ingredients make this a quick and easy pudding which can be prepared well ahead. It is made special by the use of praline, that glorious confection of nuts and burned sugar, which is so easy to make once you understand caramel making.

for 6–8 people
6–8 ripe bananas (depending on size)
3–4 pieces ginger from the syrup
3–4 tablespoons ginger syrup
10 fl oz (300 ml) whipping cream

Praline
4 oz (100 g) granulated sugar
4 tablespoons water
1½–2 oz (35–50 g) whole or flaked almonds or almonds and hazelnuts mixed

Peel and thickly slice the bananas into a shallow dish, finely chop the ginger and sprinkle it over with the syrup.

Whip the cream until stiff and spoon it over the bananas and ginger. Cover and chill. This can be made up to 24 hours ahead.

Praline. Lightly brown the almonds, and hazlenuts if used, in a moderate to hot oven or under the grill but watch and turn them for they burn very easily. Rub the hazelnut skins off by gathering them into a kitchen towel and rubbing briskly before picking out the hazelnuts, leaving behind the flakes of brown skin; set aside.

Place the sugar and water in a saucepan; you need a good pan for this because if it cannot get hot enough crystals of sugar will form around the edge and the whole lot will be in danger of crystallising. Heat gently, stirring, without letting the syrup boil until every grain of sugar has dissolved; this is most important for if some crystals remain when the mixture boils, crystallisation can be precipitated. Once dissolved, turn up the heat and boil fast without stirring (for stirring can also precipitate crystallisation), until the syrup boils to a light caramel brown. Add the nuts to the pan and continue to cook to a good brown (do not stir). Have ready an oiled piece of tinfoil on a baking sheet and very quickly (for caramel can overcook and burn in a trice) pour the praline out in a thin layer onto the tinfoil and leave to harden.

Use the double-bladed knife. Roughly break up the praline and place in the bowl; process to powdery crumbs and store in an airtight container until needed (praline will keep for several months but is nicest used fresh for it gradually stales and can end up with a horrible peppery flavour. It can also go sticky if not kept absolutely airtight).

To serve. Sprinkle a heavy layer of praline all over the whipped cream and banana and serve at once.

Alternatively, the finished dish can be shot under a pre-heated grill for about a minute for the praline to melt a bit and the cream to bubble or, to vary the flavour, a little rum or crème de cacao can be sprinkled over the bananas.

Variations
Banana, Guava and Rum Praliné. If you don't like ginger, try mixing drained guava from a 1 lb (450 g) tin and a little rum with the banana.

Pouring the hot Praline onto a sheet of greased foil

Breaking the set Praline into the Magimix

Yoghurt and Cream Topped Fruit Praliné. If your menu is a bit rich, try using 5 fl oz (150 ml) of thick plain yoghurt into which you fold 5 fl oz (150 ml) whipped double cream. Squeeze lime or lemon juice onto the bananas and mix a little grated rind into the praline.

————— : —————

Chicken Liver Tartlettes

When a hot starter seems the thing, these delicate cream cheese pastry shells, cooked and filled with a light chicken liver concoction, are an interesting though more time-consuming alternative to the Chicken Liver Pâté.

for 6–8 people
Chicken Liver Filling
8 oz (225 g) chicken livers
1 small onion
4 oz (100 g) butter
2 eggs
8 fl oz (225 ml) whipping cream
¼ teaspoon quatre épice or ground allspice
1 tablespoon brandy
1 tablespoon finely chopped parsley
a little fresh or pinch dried marjoram
salt and pepper

Cream Cheese Pastry
8 oz (225 g) plain flour
5 oz (125 g) soft butter
5 oz (125 g) cream cheese such as Eden Vale
   Somerset soft cream cheese
¼ teaspoon salt

Pastry. *Use the double-bladed knife.* Use really soft butter, or process it until really soft, for if the flour is added to an over-firm mixture and takes too long to process to a dough, tough pastry will result.

Process the butter until creamy, then add the cream cheese and process together (do not process for too long once the cream cheese has been added or you could turn it to butter). Add the flour and salt and process with the on/off technique, stopping to scrape round the bowl once or twice, until the pastry forms a pliable dough. Turn out, form into 6–8 even sized flattened balls and chill for ½–2 hours until firm enough to roll. Roll and line 6–8 (5 in/12 cm) individual tartlette tins, prick the bases, line with

The pastry is rolled into individual circles to line the tartlette tins

Taking care to press the pastry neatly into the corners

The tins are then lined with foil before they are filled with beans and baked

tinfoil, fill with baking beans and cook in a hot oven (400°F/200°C/Gas 6) for about 8–10 minutes. Remove the beans and tinfoil, turn down the oven to moderately hot (375°F/190°C/Gas 5) and continue to cook for several minutes until firm and light golden.

Pour in the chicken liver mixture and continue to bake for about 10 minutes more until just set. Do not overcook or the eggs in the mixture will go wet and grainy. Serve hot, warm or cold.

Chicken Liver Filling. *Use the double-bladed knife.* Roughly chop the onion using the on/off technique and soften gently in half the butter in a frying pan. Pick over the livers, carefully removing any green-tinged flesh and threads, and cut into 2–3 pieces. When the onion is soft, turn up the heat, add the chicken livers, sauté over high heat until sealed then add quatre épice or allspice and salt and pepper; cover and continue to cook over low heat for a few moments until the chicken livers are just cooked but still rosy inside. Turn them into the Magimix and process until smooth, adding the remaining butter, eggs, cream, brandy and herbs. Pour through a sieve and fill the pastry cases.

Chicken Liver Terrine. The chicken liver filling from the above recipe is turned into a terrine, and baked in a bain marie in a moderate oven (350°F/180°C/Gas 4) for ¾–1 hour. It is cooked until it is just firm to the touch or until a skewer plunged in comes out clean. Serve cold with bread or toast.

The Chicken Liver Filling being poured into the finished tartlette cases

—————— : ——————

Sauté of Chicken with Creamy Tomato Sauce

This is a delicate version of the Spiced Chicken with Tomato and Cheese. The seasoning mix is lighter and the chicken joints are finished and coated with a smooth, creamy sauce which immediately takes the dish into a more elegant realm.

for 6–8 people
2 chickens, cut into eight portions
   or 6–8 portions of chicken
2 tablespoons olive oil
½ oz (12 g) butter
1 lb (450 g) peeled, de-seeded and roughly chopped
   tomatoes
3–4 leaves fresh or ¼ teaspoon dried basil
1 bay leaf
10–12 fl oz (300–350 ml) double cream

Seasoning Salt
¾ teaspoon fine sea salt (ordinary salt is stronger
   so adjust)
3–4 black peppercorns
½ clove garlic
3–4 leaves fresh or ¼ teaspoon dried basil
small pinch of fennel seeds or ½ teaspoon chopped
   fresh fennel

For spicing and cooking the chicken, follow the recipe for Spiced Chicken with Tomato and Cheese (page 11).

Remove the cooked chicken portions from the sauce and keep warm. Boil up the sauce, gradually adding the double cream and reduce quickly over high heat, whilst stirring and crushing the tomatoes. When you have achieved a thick and glossy sauce (this may take up to 10 minutes, depending on your pan and stove), correct the seasoning, adding a squeeze of lemon juice if necessary.

Use the double-bladed knife. Pour the sauce into the Magimix bowl, process until smooth then pass through a sieve over the chicken joints. Serve at once.

To keep warm. Keep the un-sauced chicken warm carefully and the sauce, covered, in the pan. Only sauce the joints on serving, but beware of any juices that have come out of the chicken; add them to the sauce in the pan and, if they thin it too much, boil it again for a moment to reduce again. Should your sauce go buttery and separated from being reduced and intensified too much, you have just boiled off too much moisture; you can correct this by adding a little water, and stirring hard.

Petits Pois à la Française

This classic way with peas is marvellous; you can keep the dish warm or reheat it for a dinner party.

for 6–8 people
2 lb (900 g) shelled or thawed deep frozen petits pois
1 head shredded lettuce
2 tablespoons sugar
12 halved spring onions or 1 finely chopped onion
3–4 oz (75–100 g) butter
4–8 tablespoons water (frozen peas need the lesser amount)
salt and pepper

Melt the butter in a heavy casserole, add the onion and lettuce and toss before adding all the remaining ingredients. Cover closely and cook gently on top of the stove or in a very moderate oven (325°F/170°C/Gas 3) for 40–50 minutes until the peas are soft and tender and a little syrupy juice remains. Add more water if it all evaporates or boil fast if too much is left. Keep warm or reheat if you prefer.

Almond Shortbread Fingers

Crispy almond biscuits are nice to serve with this or any other creamy fruit pudding. They are so quick to make in the Magimix that one can hardly believe it.

40–45 biscuits
9 oz (250 g) plain flour
8 oz (225 g) butter
4 oz (100 g) castor sugar
3 oz (75 g) ground almonds
1 teaspoon almond essence

Use the double-bladed knife. Place the flour in the Magimix bowl and add in the butter, chopped into thumb nail sized cubes. Add sugar, almonds and essence then process until it all resembles fine bread crumbs. Turn into 2 12 by 10 in. (30 by 25 cm) tins, level off and press down lightly. Bake in a moderate oven (350°F/180°C/Gas 4) for about 20 minutes, until pale golden brown and cooked right through. Remove from the oven and leave for about five minutes before cutting into fingers; leave for five more minutes to firm up then remove from the tin and cool on a rack. Store in an airtight tin.

The Sauté of Chicken with Creamy Tomato Sauce decorated with watercress and ready to serve

A Summer Dinner Party

My summertime criteria are that food should not take too long to prepare and that I should be able to do it in my own time. I can then garden or lie in the sun by day and, bursting with solar energy, scamper round the kitchen in the evening. Now is not the moment for complicated recipes but a time to make the most of fresh ingredients. My other criterion is that food should not only be seasonal but should look seasonal, pretty and light, fresh and appetising, and capture the very breath of summer on a plate.

In summer you really can find fresh vegetables which will taste good with the minimum of attention.

The courgettes are firm and green, without that bitter after-taste that long-picked ones acquire. Tomatoes, hardly worth your attention in winter, are now plump and glowing and have that magic ingredient – taste – which so often seems last on the list of the grower's requirements!

I think lamb is the perfect summer meat; it now has a little more flavour than the earliest spring meat, but is still neat and delicate; it can be cooked in a flash as a cutlet, or quickly roasted in the oven. A rack is a nice little joint for two to three people, four if they are not too greedy, for you can't really get more than seven cutlets on a best end though sometimes the

MENU

Scampi Terrine with Tomato Sauce served with Melba Toast

———

Rack of Lamb
or

Guards of Honour with Herb and Nut Stuffing

New Potatoes with Mint and Parsley

Courgettes with Cream and Tarragon

———

Fresh Strawberry or Raspberry Mousse

Variations

Red Pepper Soup. A less expensive alternative to the Scampi Terrine; good hot or cold.
Prawn Toasts. These are to serve with the Red Pepper Soup or indeed with many other soups. Other suitable starters might be the **Smoked Trout Quenelles** (page 40), (if you can get watercress in summer) or any of the Informal Supper Party first courses.

———

Leg of Lamb with Saffron and Almond Sauce. An unusual alternative to the best ends of lamb and very easily kept warm. It's best served with some vegetable other than Courgettes with Cream and Tarragon which would end up too saucy and creamy.

———

Vanilla Ice Cream and Pineapple Sauce. This recipe was sparked off by a visit to the Caribbean and is good summer or winter.
Pineapple and Banana in Caramel Syrup. This gives a fresh fruit pudding for any time of year.

butcher manages to squeeze out an eighth by cutting into the shoulder. Should you need more, you can have two best ends as racks or form Guards of Honour. Lamb, whilst young and not carrying much fat, is delicious hot or cold and to me there is nothing more delicate than a cold cutlet, still a little pink, nibbled off the bone with a hint of mint jelly. As an alternative, you might like to try a Leg of Lamb, spiked with lime and gently braised with saffron, the sauce being finished off with almonds, pulverised in the Magimix. It's light and summery but can also be served in winter using more mature lamb or hogget. I would serve it with plain vegetables rather than with the Courgettes with Cream and Tarragon.

Seasonal summer fruits simply must be enjoyed while they are around and are lovely fresh on their own or with a real homemade Vanilla Ice Cream, which is also nice served with the Pineapple Sauce. But, of course, the wayward palate has only got to have fresh strawberries or raspberries from the garden for a week or two and it demands a change; in this case, make them into a fresh mousse.

The Scampi Terrine, which is incredibly quick to make in the Magimix, can be made twenty-four hours ahead, and is served with fresh Tomato Sauce. I once made the fresh tomato sauce with yellow tomatoes from the greenhouse and of course the colour threw everyone into confusion as well as completely changing the look of the dish. Another little joke on the palate is the Red Pepper Soup, looking for all the world like tomato soup. The anticipating taste buds are thrown from their expectation and have to start searching for the real flavour. It's a good soup, quick and easy to make, and can be served hot or cold with pretty summer garnishes.

Of course, you will often want to serve New Potatoes, and I always chop a bit of mint in with the parsley to bring the flavour through. The Courgettes with Cream and Tarragon are a dream, the taste still clear, clean and uncluttered or as an alternative, try stir-frying your courgettes quickly to jade green crunchiness.

Fresh herbs are my passion and at last, with a herb garden, I can use them as extravagantly as I like, which is by the handful, in the right place. If you can't get them like that, you can still make the fresh lemony, nutty stuffing for the lamb with parsley and watercress.

Make the terrine or the soup and the ice cream or the mousse the evening before. Be a little wary of preparing fresh strawberry, raspberry or pineapple with gelatine too far ahead, because sometimes the enzymes in these acidic raw fruits cause the gelatine to break down, and when you come to eat it, it may be a bit runny underneath. Get the lamb prepared by the butcher if you don't want to do it yourself. The final preparations then become very simple; prepare the stuffing, stuff the lamb and pop it in to roast; cook the vegetables lightly and reheat the soup – no great effort in even the hottest weather. If the weather looks like playing tricks on you, the menu with hot soup and hot meat and vegetables will stand up to even the most blustery of English summer days.

The prepared tomatoes and tarragon for the sauce to accompany the Scampi Terrine

Scampi Terrine with Tomato Sauce

A delicately flavoured quenelle mixture, baked in a terrine and served cold (I like to arrange a generous slice on each plate with a spoonful of tomato sauce on the side and a sprig of chervil or watercress). It is also delicious warm or hot but as it will not slice easily when hot, it is best cooked in a well buttered ring mould or soufflé dish and turned out (though you could spoon it from the dish for simplicity).

for 6–8 people
Scampi Terrine
9 oz (250 g) skinned, boned and filleted whiting
6 oz (175 g) raw un-breaded scampi (when using frozen scampi, allow a little extra weight for the ice coating which drips off as they thaw)
3 egg whites
12–15 fl oz (350–450 ml) double cream
salt, pepper and mace
sprigs chervil, watercress or parsley to garnish

Tomato Sauce
3–4 tablespoons olive oil
½ small onion
12 oz (350 g) tomatoes
1½ teaspoons tomato purée
a little grated lemon rind and juice
a little chopped fresh or pinch dried tarragon
salt and pepper

Use the double-bladed knife. Place the roughly cut up whiting and scampi in the Magimix and process until finely chopped; add the egg whites and process again until absolutely smooth. Season with salt, pepper and mace, then with the motor running, gradually add the cream, processing until you have a firm homogeneous mass; (do not process for more than about 20 seconds or you may curdle the cream). Turn into a well-oiled oblong or rectangular 1½ pint (900 ml) terrine. Cover, stand in a bain marie (a roasting pan filled with boiling water to come nearly to the full depth of the terrine) and bake in a moderate oven (350°F/180°C/Gas 4) for about 25–35 minutes until firm and a skewer comes out clean. Leave to cool, preferably for 24–48 hours, before turning out and slicing. Serve on individual plates, accompanied by a spoonful of tomato sauce and decorated with sprigs of chervil, watercress or parsley. The terrine and sauce can also be served hot.

Tomato Sauce. Warm the olive oil and gently cook the very finely chopped onion until tender but uncoloured. Peel, de-seed and dice the tomatoes, removing any tough white core from the stalk ends. Add tomatoes and purée to the pan and cook gently for several minutes before adding the chopped tarragon, lemon rind and juice and seasoning. Stir and press with a wooden spoon until you have a reduced but not too smooth sauce. Chill and serve with the terrine.

Processing the tomatoes in the Magimix makes (for my taste) too smooth a sauce for this dish.

Checking the consistency of the processed whiting and scampi

Using a zester to add the lemon rind to the tomato sauce

The completed quenelle mixture after the addition of the remaining ingredients

Rack of Lamb

Neatly butchered and prepared best ends of lamb make a lovely summer roast and you can either get your butcher to prepare them for you or do it yourself. Rack of lamb also eats extremely well cold; the skin side can be spread with your own mixture of herbs, crumbs, mustard etc. before roasting. The stuffing from the Guards of Honour recipe can, if you so wish, be formed into balls and fried to a crisp brown to accompany your rack.

for 6–8 people
2 plump best-ends of lamb (chined, 7–8 bones in
    each)
salt and pepper
1 bunch watercress to garnish

To prepare rack of lamb. If you asked for the joint to be chined, the butcher will have sawn through where the rib bones attach the backbone; with a little sharp knife, carefully remove the backbone with as little meat on it as possible. Look at one end of the best-end and you should find a thin wedge of gristly bone; this is the tip of the shoulder blade and you should carefully cut it out. Look between the skin and the meat along where the backbone was and you will see a long, whitish piece of tough cartilage; carefully remove this too. Now turn to the bone ends; these need all the meat cutting off them so they are exposed and stick out like fingers; so cut straight across the skin about 1 in. (3 cm) down the bones from the 'eye' or noix of meat, then trim off all meat and skin from each bone. If the best-ends are rather fatty, carefully pull and cut off the skin and trim off excess fat to leave no more than a ¼ in. (½ cm) layer. Lightly cut criss-cross lines in the fat to make a diamond pattern but don't cut deeply enough to cut into the meat. This allows the fat to render out during the cooking so it is deliciously crisp and not greasy and fatty. Season the fat with plenty of salt and pepper but the meaty part only with pepper (salt will draw moisture from the meat).

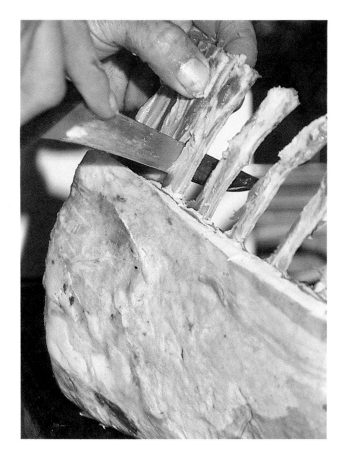

To cook rack of lamb. Pre-heat the oven to hot (400°F/200°C/Gas 6). Bring the prepared joints to room temperature before roasting and pat dry with kitchen paper if at all moist. Lay the two racks, skin-side upwards, in a roasting tin with the tips of the bones wrapped in a strip of tinfoil to stop them burning and roast for 25–35 minutes (it is difficult to be precise about the timing as racks of lamb vary in size through the year and some people like it pinker than others). Now rest the meat for 15–30 minutes, or even longer, before serving, garnished with watercress. It must rest in a warm place (turned off oven, warming drawer, etc.) where it cannot possibly cook any more. The temperature should be not more than 200°F/100°C/Gas ¼. This allows the meat fibres to relax and the juices to re-enter the tissues, making it more succulent and tender. It also means you have no last minute worries and it does not matter when you eat.

Guards of Honour

In this rather special dish, two prepared racks of lamb are tied together, with the bones interlaced to simulate the archway of swords used by a military guard of honour outside a church. You can cook it with the fresh, herby stuffing packed between the two racks or leave out the stuffing altogether. Balance the herbs carefully, using far less of the powerful tarragon, thyme and rosemary than of the chervil and parsley which can be thrown in with relative abandon.

for 6–8 people
2 plump (7–8 bone) best ends of lamb prepared as
    for Rack of Lamb above
salt and pepper
1 bunch watercress to garnish

The three photographs on the left show the preparation of a Rack of Lamb and the two photographs on the right show the Guards of Honour being stuffed and tied

Herb and Nut Stuffing
2 oz (50 g) butter
2 shallots or 1 small onion
1 bunch watercress
1 handful fresh mixed herbs such as parsley, chervil,
    tarragon, thyme and rosemary (or you can use
    2 bunches of watercress)
1 oz (25 g) suet (optional)
4 oz (100 g) stale brown or white bread
2 oz (50 g) walnut halves
½ clove garlic
grated rind of ½ lemon
1 egg
salt, pepper and mace

Herb and Nut Stuffing. Finely chop the shallot or onion and fry gently to soften in the butter.
Use the double-bladed knife. Tear the bread up into the Magimix bowl and process to coarse breadcrumbs; set aside. Roughly chop the nuts and set

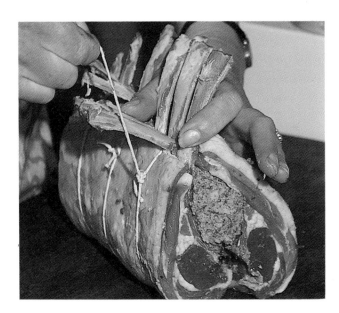

The cooked Guards of Honour with the Courgettes with Cream and Tarragon

aside. Remove and discard the tough stalks from the watercress and herbs. Finely chop the herbs then add the softened onions and butter to the bowl with the suet, breadcrumbs, chopped walnuts, crushed garlic and lemon rind. Season with salt, pepper and mace and add an egg. Process with the on/off technique until amalgamated, but not for too long or the stuffing becomes too tight and solid.

Prepare a matching pair of best ends as for the Rack of Lamb (page 22). Then pack the stuffing between the concave bone sides of the racks, standing them upright with the bones slotted through each other like entwined fingers. Now tie them with string in two or three places to hold them together and wrap the tips of the bones in a strip of tinfoil to stop them burning.

Cook as for Racks of Lamb but stand the lamb bones upwards and roast for 35–45 minutes, depending on their size. Rest before carving as above and serve garnished with watercress.

New Potatoes with Mint and Parsley

Well flavoured new potatoes need very little dressing up but the classic addition of parsley and mint brings out the best in them.

for 6–8 people
2½–3 lb (1.15–1.35 kg) baby new potatoes
2 good sprigs of mint
a handful of parsley
2 oz (50 g) butter
salt and pepper

Rub or scrape the skins off the potatoes and bring a pan of water to the boil. Salt the water and add the potatoes with one of the sprigs of mint and the stem of the other, having picked the leaves off it first. While the potatoes boil, and they may take 12–20 minutes depending on size, chop the parsley and mint leaves.

Use the double-bladed knife. Place the head of parsley, stalks removed, and mint leaves in the Magimix and chop finely.

When the potatoes are done, drain them into a colander and remove the boiled mint; wipe out the saucepan then add the butter, cut into small pieces; heat until bubbling and then return the potatoes to the pan, season lightly and add the chopped parsley and mint. Toss around until the potatoes are well coated in butter and chopped herbs and turn into a serving dish.

———— : ————

Courgettes with Cream and Tarragon

A lovely different way with courgettes and good with a roast, grill or 'dry' meat dish because of its creamy consistency. You can grate and salt the courgettes to draw out their moisture but I often pick them from the garden, grate them, wring them out in a clean cloth and we are eating them within a quarter of an hour of picking.

Grating the courgettes

for 6–8 people
1½–2 lb (675–900 g) courgettes
2 tablespoons olive oil
2 oz (50 g) butter
a little chopped fresh or a good pinch of dried
    tarragon
5 tablespoons double or whipping cream
good squeeze lemon juice
salt and pepper

Use the coarse grating disc. Grate the courgettes. To remove excess moisture, turn the grated courgettes into a piece of muslin or a clean kitchen cloth; screw up tightly and squeeze out any liquid. Heat the oil and butter in a wok or frying pan until it is sizzling then add the courgettes and chopped tarragon and stir fry for 3–5 minutes until just tender. Add the cream and season fairly highly; boil for several minutes until it makes a nice creamy sauce and finish with a good squeeze of lemon juice.

Fresh Strawberry or Raspberry Mousse

This is one of those cheaty quick Magimix recipes which breaks all the rules and still wins. Just right for a hot day when you don't want to spend too long in the kitchen, though of course you can use frozen fruit for this in the winter. If you want to sieve out the pips, you can do so and you can, if you wish, whip the cream separately and fold it into the mousse to give you a lighter and arguably better result. But I am showing the high speed Magimix way for when you are in a hurry.

for 6–8 people
1 lb (450 g) strawberries or raspberries
6 oz (175 g) castor sugar or to taste
4 fl oz (100 ml) boiling water
3½ teaspoons gelatine
10 fl oz (300 ml) double or whipping cream
4 egg whites
3 tablespoons raspberry liqueur or eau-de-vie or
    kirsch (optional)

Frozen strawberries or raspberries need to be thoroughly thawed before using for if they are very cold, the gelatine can set too quickly and go stringy.
Use the double-bladed knife. Place the gelatine and the boiling water in the bowl, switch on and process until melted; then add the sugar and process for 10 seconds. Now add the berries and process until absolutely smooth before pouring in the cream. Once the cream is added, only process for about 20 seconds to thicken the cream; too long and it can turn to butter. (You can, if you wish, whip the cream by hand and fold in with the egg whites). Set the mixture aside for a few minutes until cold and beginning to thicken then, in a separate bowl, whisk the egg whites until just holding a peak and fold in the fruit mixture. Turn into a 2 pint (1.2 l) soufflé dish and chill until set.

Pouring the boiling water onto the gelatine in the Magimix bowl

Adding the fruit mixture to the whipped egg whites

The Strawberry Mousse decorated for that special occasion ▶

Red Pepper Soup

A slightly unusual velvety soup which is good hot or cold. It is rather nice served with a few ice cubes, prawns, with wafer thin slices of lime floating in it and hot prawn toasts to accompany it.

for 6–8 people
about 1½–2 lb (675–900 g) sweet red peppers
1 large onion
2 oz (50 g) butter
1 tablespoon tomato purée
2 oz (50 g) plain flour
3½ pints (2 l) chicken stock
2 teaspoons fresh or ¼ teaspoon dried basil or
    marjoram (less of the annual marjoram which is
    very powerful)
good squeeze lime or lemon juice
salt and pepper

To serve cold
6 fl oz (175 ml) whipping or single cream
extra lime or lemon juice to taste
wafer slices of lime
a few peeled prawns or shreds of red pepper
a few ice cubes
a sprinkle fresh chopped basil, marjoram or parsley

Use the standard slicing disc. Cut the peppers in half, remove the stalk, seeds and white core, pack into the feed tube and slice, followed by the peeled onion. Add them to the melted butter in a large saucepan, cover and gently cook for 20–30 minutes until the peppers are soft and the onion is golden, but not brown. Stir in the tomato purée and fry for several minutes, before stirring in the flour. Add the stock and bring to the boil whisking well, then season and simmer for 10 minutes or so.

Use the double-bladed knife. Strain the soup and process the solids in the Magimix; when absolutely smooth, pour some of the reserved liquid down the feed tube while the machine is running. Pour the soup through a sieve back into the rinsed out pan and add the remaining stock. Chop the herbs finely and add them together with a good squeeze of lime or lemon juice. Correct the seasoning, reheat and serve accompanied by hot prawn toasts.

To serve cold. Make sure you do not use too rich a jellied chicken stock or you will find yourself serving a thick red pepper porridge and cut the flour quantity by about ½ oz (12 g) as it will thicken more as it cools. When cold, add plenty of lime or lemon juice to taste, the cream and cracked ice cubes. Serve in individual bowls, garnished with wafer thin slices of lime, shreds of red pepper, a sprinkle of fresh herbs and a few chopped prawns if you like. Hand hot Prawn Toasts separately.

Halving and de-seeding the red peppers

Using the standard slicing disc to slice both the peppers and onion

Pouring some of the liquid onto the cooked and puréed pepper mixture

Ice cold Red Pepper Soup with a plate of hot Prawn Toasts ▶

Prawn Toasts

Fried fingers of bread with a spicy prawn filling.

for 6–8 people
6–8 slices thin cut stale bread
6 oz (175 g) prawns
1 egg white
1 teaspoon anchovy essence
¾ teaspoon curry powder
a few small sprigs of parsley
¼ teaspoon pounded coriander
a little grated fresh root ginger (optional)
good squeeze lemon juice
salt and pepper
oil for deep frying

Use the double-bladed knife. Process the prawns until chopped, add the white of egg and all the flavourings and process to a paste. Remove the crusts from the bread, spread the mixture over half the slices and top with the remaining slices; press well together and cut each slice into four fingers. Deep fry in hot oil until crisp and golden brown; drain well on kitchen paper and set aside. Reheat in a moderate oven (350°F/180°C/Gas 4) for 10 minutes or so before serving.

Leg of Lamb with Saffron and Almond Sauce

This long and gently cooked leg of lamb, with its creamy almond and saffron sauce, will keep warm perfectly, has a lovely delicate flavour and great tenderness. Only use limes or lemons with a thin skin for those with a thick white pith will introduce a bitter note. If these are all I can get, I shave off the outer skin to slice and use, trim away and discard the white pith, then I slice and use the inner fruit.

for 6–8 people
4–6 lb (1.8–2.7 kg) leg of lamb
1 lime or thin skinned lemon (not with a heavy white pith)
1 tablespoon olive oil
2 oz (50 g) butter
1 packet saffron
½–¾ pint (300–450 ml) stock (chicken is fine or stock cube and water)
1 sliced onion
4 oz (100 g) whole blanched almonds
salt and pepper

Take half the lime or lemon, cut into 3–4 wafer thin slices then cut these into quarters. Slip these slices

The ingredients for the Prawn Toast filling

Spreading the processed mixture onto the bread slices

into little slits in the lamb, especially around the bone. Soak the saffron in the heated stock. Heat the oil and butter in a frying pan or casserole and gently brown the leg of lamb on all sides with the sliced onion for 10 minutes or so. Add the saffron stock to the casserole (if using a frying pan, turn all into a casserole or covered dish at this stage, not forgetting to rinse out the tasty bits from the frying pan with the stock). Season lightly, cover and cook gently in a very moderate oven (325°F/170°C/Gas 3) for 2½–3½ hours until tender.

Use the double-bladed knife. Process the almonds until very smooth then gradually add the stock and onion from the lamb (having removed some excess fat) to make a very smooth sauce. Pass through a fine sieve; better still, to get a velvet smooth sauce, turn the sauce into a sieve, lined with a large square of double thickness muslin, then literally squeeze the sauce through the muslin which will catch the gritty almond. Add a little grated lime or lemon rind and a good squeeze of juice to the sauce. Correct seasoning and reheat sauce gently to boiling point; the almonds will thicken in the same way as a flour based sauce. Serve the sauce with the carved lamb. This will keep warm very well, with the sauce in a bain marie and the lamb in the casserole in a warm place.

———— : ————

Vanilla Ice Cream and Pineapple Sauce

Home made vanilla ice cream is lovely in summer time with strawberries and raspberries. At other times, you might like to try serving it with this fresh pineapple and caramel sauce which is flavoured with crème de cacao or rum and spiked with cardamom to give extra interest and take the edge off its sweetness.

for 6–8 people
Vanilla Ice Cream
15 fl oz (450 ml) milk
3 egg yolks
7 oz (200 g) sugar
1 vanilla pod and vanilla essence to taste
8 fl oz (225 ml) whipping cream
⅛ teaspoon salt

Pineapple Sauce
1 pineapple
6 oz (175 g) granulated sugar
6 tablespoons cold water
3 fl oz (75 ml) boiling water
2–3 tablespoons crème de cacao or rum
2–3 cardamom pods

Vanilla Ice Cream. Pour the milk into a saucepan and heat to just below boiling point. Place the egg yolks and sugar in the bowl, process to mix, then with the machine running, pour the hot milk in through the feed tube. Make a custard by cooking the egg mixture, to which you have added the vanilla pod either in a bowl (not pyrex in which custards never thicken) over hot water, a double saucepan or in a heavy pan over direct heat (but not aluminium which discolours egg mixtures). Heat gently, stirring, until the mixture lightly coats the back of a spoon, but do not let it boil or the eggs will curdle. Cool, then remove the vanilla pod and add vanilla essence and cream. When cold, turn the mixture into a shallow container (preferably tinfoil or metal as these conduct cold well) and freeze, stirring the edges into the middle from time to time.

Use the double-bladed knife. When almost frozen, turn into the Magimix and process until smooth; turn into a box and keep in the freezer. Mellow in the fridge for half an hour before serving.

Pineapple Sauce. Place the sugar and cold water in a saucepan and dissolve the sugar, stirring, over gentle heat. Once every grain of sugar has dissolved, turn up the heat and boil fast to a good brown caramel. Have the boiling water ready and add to the caramel on the stove (beware – it splutters). Boil until all the caramel dissolves and you have a heavy syrup. Cool.

Use the double-bladed knife. Peel, quarter lengthways, core and roughly cut the pineapple into the Magimix and process until fairly finely chopped. Add the cooled syrup, crème de cacao or rum and the cardamom pods, shelled and crushed in a mortar, and process again briefly. Serve cold as a sauce with the ice cream.

Variation
Pineapple and Banana in Caramel Syrup. Make the caramel syrup above and add the juice of a lemon, the pounded cardamom and crème de cacao or rum if you wish. Stir in cubes of fresh pineapple and 2–3 bananas, cut into generous chunks. On serving, if the syrup is too heavy, add a drop of water.

A Winter Dinner Party

———— ◆ ————

The dull weather and indoor feeling of the long winter months is a marvellous moment in which to have a dinner party. Your friends will like being entertained and cheered up and really appreciate being asked out. I enjoy cooking in winter; it's no pain to be tucked up warm in the kitchen and I am not longing to be out of doors.

Winter food should suit the season with warm rich dishes that satisfy and wafting smells to tickle the nose. I like to use seasonal vegetables, which seem to suit the winter months better than summer ones from the freezer, and as much colour as possible to cheer up what can be a rather drab time of year. With many of us working in centrally heated offices, few of us actually need the hefty calories of old-fashioned winter food so it's really the illusion of heavy food we are trying to create.

I might start with a Hot Beetroot Soup with its wonderful colour and rich aroma; because we strain out the beetroot it's not too rustic (the bits can be left in to make a hearty supper dish on other occasions) and, if it is served with sour cream and caviar croûtes, it becomes positively sophisticated. As an alternative, and equally suitable in a summer menu, I might think of Smoked Trout Quenelles with Watercress Sauce, light and delicate in flavour, the pinky quenelles contrasting with the fresh green sauce. Sometimes a winter menu can look a little dull, especially by candlelight, so this is the sort of thing I look for to brighten it up. Watercress is at its best and most flavoursome in winter but is sometimes difficult to get in very hard weather or at the back end, so be prepared for a last minute change.

For special occasions, nothing is better than whole Roast Fillet of Beef, served with Béarnaise Butter. The flavourings of Béarnaise sauce, whipped by the Magimix into butter and cream, make a delicious and easily prepared alternative to classic Béarnaise. Alternatively, and rather less expensively, how about the Leg of Lamb with Saffron and Almond Sauce (page 30). For a seasonal vegetable, a Gratin of Potato, Carrot and Celeriac is attractive and means you don't need to offer any other vegetable. If you prefer to have little button sprouts, they would add extra colour and crunch to the plate or, in late winter when they get rather big and open, turn them into Créme de Bruxelles which seems to be enjoyed by even the most avid sprout-hater! In this case, you will need a potato so I suggest Magimix Potato Galette, a crisp, brown-coated potato cake.

Chestnut Pudding is a firm winter favourite and using tinned chestnut purée is so quick and easy in the Magimix. Fresh chestnuts, which really do taste better than tinned, are in season from November until just after Christmas and, though a bit tiresome to prepare, are well worth the effort.

Fresh pineapple from South Africa takes us nearly to Christmas when the Caribbean fruit takes over. Make it into a Fresh Pineapple Tart (page 132) with a rum flavoured, cream cheese mixture beneath it and lightly glazed on top. Another idea is cubes of pineapple, smothered with cream and praline. If that's too rich for you and you feel you need a light refreshing finish, how about ice cream with Pineapple Sauce (page 31). Any of these would make a fitting finish to a winter feast.

To gild the lily a little, everyone really enjoys a plate of hot, crisp and really cheesy straws, handed round at the end of dinner (but not of course if you have used pastry in the pudding). Just occasionally I may feel like making some petits fours or Almond and Raisin Balls to have with our coffee, though it's

MENU

Hot Beetroot Soup with Sour Cream and Caviar Croûtes

Roast Fillet of Beef with Béarnaise Butter

Gratin of Potato, Carrot and Celeriac

Chestnut Pudding

Variations

Smoked Trout Quenelles with Watercress Sauce. A classic dish made from ingredients now available all the year round and a lovely idea for a first course if you like to start with fish.

Crème de Bruxelles. An unusual and delicious way to use brussels sprouts.
Magimix Potato Galette. This is so handy for a dinner party because it needs no last minute attention.

Fresh Pineapple Tart. (page 132) A beautiful looking pudding, variable according to the season and your fancy and suitable for so many occasions.
Cheese Straws. Everyone loves these as a savoury or, cut smaller, to go with your apéritif.
Almond and Raisin Balls. Homemade sweets for after dinner.

Nicola and Simon Cox giving a dinner party at Farthinghoe

more often the after eights or the chocolate matchsticks. I have included the recipe for Almond and Raisin Balls, they are very easy to make in the Magimix, and also ideal as small Christmas presents or for your husband's stocking.

Grating the raw beetroot

The Hot Beetroot soup has a marvellous and warm colour

Hot Beetroot Soup with Sour Cream and Caviar Croûtes

A clear beetroot consommé with a lovely bright ruby colour, especially when you use round beetroots whose colour is so much better than the long varieties. Good stock is needed, but I'm afraid we often use tins of consommé; this and the barley give texture to the soup and the stock cube stock makes up the volume. The garnish of sour cream and caviar croûtes just adds the sort of dash that transforms this into a dinner party dish.

for 6–8 people
1½ lb (675 g) uncooked beetroot (round varieties for preference)
4 pints (2.25 l) good beef stock or use 2 tins Campbell's consommé, 3 pints (1.7 l) water and 2 beef stock cubes (Knorr)
2 oz (50 g) smoked bacon
1 large onion
½ oz (12 g) or 2 tablespoons duck, goose or chicken fat, pork dripping or oil
1–2 sticks celery
1 clove garlic
3 tablespoons pearl barley
2 tablespoons wine vinegar
bouquet garni of parsley stalks, thyme, bayleaf and 2 cloves
1 tablespoon sugar
1 tablespoon finely chopped parsley (optional)
a little fresh chopped or ⅛ teaspoon dried dill (optional)
½–1 lemon or vinegar to taste
salt and pepper

Sour Cream and Caviar Croûtes
6–8 slices stale french bread
5 fl oz (150 ml) whipping cream
lemon juice to taste
2 oz (50 g) jar danish caviar (lumpfish roe)
chopped chives or very finely chopped shallot
cayenne pepper
olive oil and butter for frying or goose fat, duck fat or good dripping

Use the double-bladed knife. Add the roughly cut up onion to the Magimix bowl and finely chop with the on/off technique. Heat the fat or oil in a heavy saucepan or casserole, dice the bacon, add with the onion and fry to a good brown, sprinkling over the sugar to help get a good colour. It is the really caramelised onions that give such flavour to this soup, so allow them time to brown really well.

Change to the fine or coarse grating disc. Peel and grate the beetroot and the celery sticks; add them, with the stock and pearl barley, to the browned onions. Flatten the clove of garlic and add with the vinegar and a bouquet garni. The bouquet need not be wrapped in muslin, for everything is drained out of the soup; on the other hand, should you wish to use the beetroot up as a simple vegetable, you would not want to be picking out all those herbs. Simmer the soup for 30–40 minutes then strain or, better still, leave to stand for some hours or overnight before straining. If the colour is not good enough, grate another beetroot into the hot soup and leave to stand for one hour then strain again. Reheat and stir in the finely chopped parsley and dill, correct the seasoning and add lemon juice or vinegar to achieve a nice, quite sour taste. Serve with the croûtes handed separately.

Sour Cream and Caviar Croûtes. Heat the fat and fry the slices of french bread to a golden brown on each side; drain on kitchen paper. Add lemon juice to taste to the cream and whisk until holding its shape. Pile onto the croûtes, cover lavishly with danish caviar and sprinkle with chopped chives or shallot and a dust of cayenne pepper. Serve with the soup. Do not prepare too long beforehand.

The finishing touch of sour cream and caviar croûtes add real elegance to the dinner party

Roast Fillet of Beef with Béarnaise Butter

Even if you can't afford the fillet, try the Béarnaise butter! It's delicious with any roast beef, is wonderful in cold beef (or ham) sandwiches and turns a baked potato into a feast. A Magimix will whip up these light creamy flavoured butters with such ease.

for 6–8 people
2½–3½ lb (1.15–1.6 kg) centre-cut fillet of beef or the whole fillet
2 tablespoons olive oil
3 oz (75 g) butter
4–6 thin cut rashers streaky bacon
salt and pepper
1 bunch watercress (to garnish)

Béarnaise Butter
4 tablespoons white wine vinegar
4 tablespoons dry white wine
3 tablespoons finely chopped shallots
1 tablespoon fresh chopped or 1 teaspoon dried tarragon
1 teaspoon fresh or ½ teaspoon dried chervil
8 oz (225 g) soft, best butter
2–3 fl oz (50–75 ml) whipping cream
1 tablespoon finely chopped, mixed fresh tarragon and chervil or parsley
salt and pepper

Trim the fillet which (unless you are using the whole fillet) should be a nice thick centre-cut of meat, well marbled with fat. Remove all external fat, strips of gristle and bluish membrane. Tie with string in 2–3 places to keep a good shape, doubling under the thin tail piece when using a whole fillet. Bring the meat to

Slicing perfectly cooked Fillet of Beef

room temperature and pat quite dry with kitchen paper. Season with pepper only (salt draws moisture from meat). Heat the oil and butter in a roasting tin on the stove and, when very hot, brown the meat all over for 5–6 minutes. Now cover the meat with thin fatty rashers of streaky bacon and, when you're ready to cook it, transfer the meat to a hot oven (425°F/220°C/Gas 7) and roast for approximately 18–25 minutes. A fillet should be basted every five minutes, but I find that by putting the bacon on, I can dispense with that and baste only once or twice. Once cooked, let the meat rest in a switched off oven or warming cupboard for from ten minutes to an hour, but make sure it is not too hot or it may continue to cook. Carve, either into thick steaks or

into thin slices, pour over the butter-gravy from the roasting pan and garnish with watercress. Serve the Béarnaise Butter separately.

Béarnaise Butter. *Use the double-bladed knife.* Combine the vinegar, wine, shallots, tarragon and chervil in a pan and simmer gently until the shallots are cooked and only about 1½ tablespoons of liquid remain (add a little water if it boils dry before the shallots are tender). Cool. Chop the butter into the Magimix and process to cream really well, before gradually adding the complete shallot reduction, followed by the cream, seasoning and finally the fresh herbs. Stop processing when you have a light creamy butter mixture. Turn into a bowl and serve soft, at kitchen temperature, with the fillet.

The various stages of making the Béarnaise Butter

Gratin of Potato, Carrot and Celeriac

I use the french fry disc, which has all sorts of uses other than just making chips, for this dish, and the vegetables are then briefly fried, layered and baked in a creamy sauce. This makes a wonderful, all-in-one vegetable which keeps warm beautifully and the creamy consistency makes it just right to accompany winter roasts and grills.

for 6–8 people
1 lb (450 g) peeled celeriac
1 lb (450 g) peeled carrot
1 lb (450 g) peeled potatoes
2 onions
3 oz (75 g) butter or dripping
1 teaspoon sugar
salt and pepper

Sauce
1 oz (25 g) butter
1 oz (25 g) flour
1 pint (600 ml) milk
3–4 oz (75–100 g) grated cheddar cheese
salt, pepper and nutmeg

Use the standard slicing disc. Slice the onion and soften in a quarter of the butter; set aside.
Use the french fry disc. Cut the celeriac, carrot and potato with firm pressure on the plunger, stacking the carrot sideways in the tube and keeping each vegetable separate. Add another quarter of the fat to the pan and toss the celeriac in the hot fat for several minutes; mix in some onion, season and turn into the bottom of a deep buttered gratin dish. Add another quarter of the fat to the pan and when hot, toss in the carrot, sprinkle with sugar and cook for 4–5 minutes (to end up cooked evenly, the carrots need to fry a little longer than the other vegetables). Mix in some of the onion, season and pack on top of the celeriac. Heat remaining fat and cook the potato sticks for several minutes before seasoning and adding in the rest of the onion; pack on top of the carrots. Pour over the sauce (it should come nearly level with the top of the vegetables), scatter generously with cheese and bake in a moderately hot oven (375°F/190°C/Gas 5), standing the dish in a bain marie, for 45–60 minutes. This will keep warm very well or can be lightly cooked and then reheated

The French Fry disc cuts the vegetables to a perfect size for the Gratin of Potato, Carrot and Celeriac

(cover with tinfoil for the first cooking so the cheese does not over-brown) in a moderate oven (350°F/180°C/Gas 4) for about 40 minutes.
Sauce. Melt the butter in a saucepan, add the flour and cook over moderate heat for several minutes; draw to the side of the stove and when the sizzling ceases, add the milk; bring to the boil whisking hard, simmer for 1–2 minutes and season with salt, pepper and nutmeg.

———————— : ————————

Chestnut Pudding

Made with a tin of chestnut purée, preferably Clément Faugier which is of the right consistency whilst some others are rather soft, this must be one of the quickest puddings to prepare and one of the most delicious. But make it with fresh chestnuts and I think you will taste the difference.

for 6–8 people

24 or so good chestnuts or 1 lb (450 g) unsweetened
    chestnut purée (Clément Faugier for choice)
6 oz (175 g) vanilla sugar or castor sugar and
    ¼ teaspoon vanilla essence
3 oz (75 g) soft lightly salted butter
½ teaspoon vanilla essence
3 tablespoons rum
8 fl oz (225 ml) whipping cream

Crème Chantilly

6 fl oz (175 ml) whipping cream
vanilla sugar to taste or castor sugar and vanilla
    essence
2 oz (50 g) good dark chocolate like Bournville,
    Terry's or Menier

Fresh chestnuts need shelling by cutting halfway round the skin of the chestnut at the waist on the rounded side. Then drop a few at a time into boiling water; boil for about 3 minutes and remove, one at a time, to peel off the outer and inner skins together. If you get it just right, one squeeze and they should just pop out. Simmer the peeled chestnuts in about ¾ pint (450 ml) of water to which you have added a vanilla pod, or a few drops of essence, for about 15–20 minutes or until they are tender. Then drain, reserving the liquid.

Use the double-bladed knife. Process the chestnuts in the Magimix until absolutely smooth, adding cooking liquid, if necessary, to make a firm purée. When cool, process in the butter. If using tinned purée, start by creaming the butter really well (if it's not really soft, the finished pudding will have a flecked texture) then add in the roughly cut up purée and process again. Add the sugar, vanilla and rum then, with the machine running, pour in the whipping cream and process for no longer than about 20 seconds (or you may turn the cream to butter) to thicken. Turn into a bowl and chill to thicken further. Spoon over a soft veil of Crème Chantilly and sprinkle heavily with grated chocolate. You can serve the Magimix Chocolate Sauce (page 103) with this; delicious but perhaps rather masking the delicate flavour of the chestnuts.

Crème Chantilly. Sweeten the cream with a little vanilla sugar and whisk, preferably with a balloon whisk, until light and airy. Pile onto the pudding.

Grated Chocolate. *Use the coarse grating disc.* Stack the chocolate upright in the feed tube (a piece from a big block is better than a very thin bar) and grate with firm pressure. Scatter over the Crème Chantilly on top of the pudding.

The Chestnut pudding can be decorated with chocolate leaves. Make these by thickly painting melted chocolate over the back of fresh leaves, rose leaves are especially suitable, then leaving the chocolate to harden before peeling off the leaf

Smoked Trout Quenelles with Watercress Sauce

The fresh trout gives texture and the smoked ones flavour to these delicate light quenelles which are so easy to whip up in the Magimix. If the idea of poaching quenelles by the spoonful daunts you, you can always pack the mixture into a ring mould and steam it! The light cream sauce has no thickening and is just a reduction of cream, flavoured with fresh watercress purée.

for 6–8 people
1 lb (450 g) fresh trout or 10 oz (275 g) filleted trout flesh
1 lb (450 g) smoked trout or 10 oz (275 g) filleted flesh
3 egg whites
10–12 fl oz (300–350 ml) double cream
a good pinch mace
salt and pepper

Watercress Sauce
4 bunches watercress
4–6 tablespoons very finely chopped shallot or onion
½ chicken stock cube
5 fl oz (150 ml) dry white wine
15 fl oz (450 ml) whipping cream or half double and half whipping
lemon juice to taste
1½–2 oz (35–50 g) butter
salt and pepper

Use the double-bladed knife. Fillet, skin and bone the trout and roughly chop into the bowl. Process the fish until smooth and then add the egg whites. When absolutely smooth, season with salt, pepper and mace and then, with the machine running, pour in the cream. Do not process for more than 20 seconds (or the cream may turn to butter) and do not add so much cream that the mixture thins and will not sit up

The preparation and poaching of the Quenelles; note how they float to the top of the pan

on a spoon. Chill mixture for 30 minutes before cooking quenelles. Bring a wide pan of salted water to the simmer. Dip a dessert spoon in warm water and take a good rounded spoonful of the quenelle mixture; shape if necessary with another wet spoon and lower into the water (tap the spoon on the bottom to detach the quenelles). Continue forming the quenelles and poach them for 8–10 minutes, carefully turning once with a slotted spoon, until just firm. Remove with a slotted spoon and drain on kitchen paper. Place in a warmed buttered gratin dish, pour over the sauce and serve at once. They can be kept warm for a while, well covered but un-sauced.

Sauce. Place the very finely chopped shallot in a small pan with the wine and simmer gently for 15–30 minutes until it is a soft purée and the wine almost gone; now add the stock cube and cream, season lightly and boil until reduced by about one third and coating a spoon; keep warm at this stage if necessary.

Meanwhile pick over the watercress, discarding the tough stalks, and toss into a pan of boiling water with 1 tablespoon of salt added. Blanch for 2–3 minutes then drain and refresh under the cold tap. Squeeze excess water out by hand.

Use the double-bladed knife. Process the watercress for 1–2 minutes until an absolutely smooth purée forms. This purée can be quickly wrapped, by the spoonful, into airtight cling film and kept refrigerated or frozen, ready to add to the prepared sauce. This is useful when watercress is unobtainable or when you want the minimum last minute work.

Now pour the hot reduced cream sauce onto the watercress purée and process, adding lemon juice to taste and butter in little bits. Pre-puréed watercress can just be whisked into the sauce with the lemon juice and flakes of butter. Strain and reheat without boiling, correct the seasoning and pour over the quenelles. Use *at once* or the colour will go dull.

With the Magimix working pour the hot cream through the feed tube onto the puréed watercress

The pretty effect given by the contrasting colours of the Quenelles and the Watercress Sauce

Crème de Bruxelles

This creamy sprout purée, useful when sprouts are not as tightly curled as they might be, usually has everyone guessing.

for 6–8 people
1½–2 lb (675–900 g) sprouts
3–4 oz (75–100 g) butter
3–4 fl oz (75–100 ml) whipping cream
freshly grated nutmeg
salt and pepper

Boil the sprouts in plenty of well salted water until just tender, then drain. Heat the cream and diced up butter until melted and hot.
Use the double-bladed knife. Process the sprouts in the Magimix, adding seasoning, nutmeg to taste and the hot butter and cream to make a spooning purée (you will have to do this in several batches if using the standard Magimix). Turn into a hot dish and serve at once or cover and keep warm.

—————— : ——————

Magimix Potato Galette

Potato dishes that need no last minute attention are so useful, especially for dinner parties. This crisp and golden grated potato cake will cook in the oven for ¾ hour or so with minimum attention before being turned out and served in wedges.

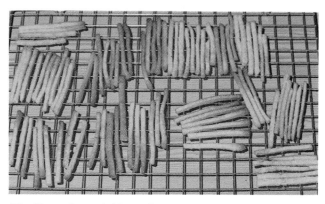

The Cheese Straws laid to cool on a rack

for 6–8 people
3–3½ lb (1.35–1.6 kg) peeled potatoes
2 tablespoons olive oil
2–3 oz (50–75 g) butter
salt and pepper

Use the coleslaw disc. Grate the potatoes, using firm pressure on the plunger. Turn them into a large bowl of cold water and leave to soak for no more than 5–10 minutes to remove some of the starch. While they soak heat half the oil and half the butter in each of two 8 in. (20 cm) non-stick cake tins.

Drain the potato shreds and dry on a clean kitchen cloth; turn them into the hot fat in the cake tins, season with salt and pepper and toss around until coated in fat; then press down to make a firm cake. Cook uncovered in a hot oven (425°F/220°C/Gas 7) for about ¾ hour until they are cooked and have a crisp brown coating. They will keep warm but are best served crispy from the hot oven, turned out onto a plate and cut into wedges.

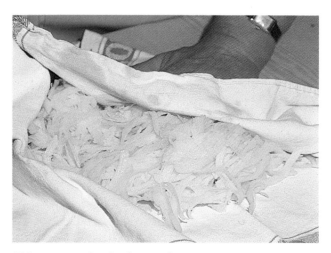

Using a tea towel to dry the grated potatoes

The crisp and brown Potato Galette on a plate and ready to slice

Cheese Straws

Generously cheesy and generously cut hot cheese straws, handed round at the end of dinner as a semi-savoury are usually pretty popular. So are a dish of them, cut smaller, with drinks. Mrs Beeton did not have a Magimix but her basic recipe cannot be bettered although it does rely on good strong cheddar, probably easier to find in her day than in ours!

about 60 straws
3 oz (75 g) butter
3 oz (75 g) plain flour
2 oz (50 g) strong cheddar
1 oz (25 g) freshly grated parmesan
1 egg yolk
2 teaspoons cold water
pinch of cayenne
pinch of salt

Use the fine grating disc. Grate the cheddar cheese. *Change to the double-bladed knife.* Add the flour and diced butter to the Magimix bowl with the parmesan cheese and seasonings and process to the bread-crumb stage before adding the egg yolk and water and processing to a stiff paste. Turn onto a floured board, knead briefly into a flat disc and roll out thinly into a rectangle 12×4 in. (30×10 cm) and 1/8 in. (3 mm) thick; cut into strips 4 in. (10 cm) long and 1/4 in. (1/2 cm) wide. Bake in a hot oven (400°F/200°C/Gas 6) for about 10–15 minutes until golden brown and crisp. Cool on a rack and keep in an airtight tin. Serve hot or cold.

Almond and Raisin Balls

These quite delicious almondy, fruity chocolate balls are so easy to make with the Magimix and are perfect to offer at the end of any dinner party, or to give away as presents. Culpepers the herbalists have lovely natural essences including almond, orange.

25 balls or so
1½ oz (35 g) almonds
1½ oz (35 g) hazelnuts
3 oz (75 g) sultanas
3 oz (75 g) raisins
grated rind of 1 orange
few drops pure almond essence
2–3 drops pure orange essence (optional)
3 oz (75 g) good dark chocolate
powdered drinking chocolate or cocoa (optional)

Brown the almonds and hazelnuts in the oven or under a grill but watch, for they burn very easily; then rub the skins off the hazelnuts in a kitchen towel. Melt the chocolate on a saucer over hot water. *Use the double-bladed knife.* Place everything in the Magimix and process until chopped and combined. Form into small balls and roll in drinking chocolate if you wish. Drop into little petit four cases if you have got them, or otherwise leave to firm up on grease-proof paper. Serve with the coffee.

All the ingredients for the Almond and Raisin Balls are placed in the Magimix before processing

Some help in the kitchen

A Sunday Lunch Party

A relaxed Sunday lunch party for family or friends is one of the nicest ways to entertain. It shouldn't involve too complicated a menu because you don't want to spend your whole weekend cooking; so I usually try to include a roast, which seems such a typical English Sunday dish and is always greatly appreciated, especially by people who live on their own or as a couple and don't often have a large roast; smaller joints, however good the quality of the meat, never really roast quite as well. With roast beef I might serve Béarnaise Butter (page 37), not the classic recipe but very good.

If you choose lamb, Guards of Honour are best, if you aren't too great a number. For a bigger party, I would turn to a crown roast or roast leg of lamb. I might be very unconventional and serve it with a Saffron and Almond Sauce or perhaps, in winter, with thick sliced onion in a cream sauce. The stuffing I use in Guards of Honour is also delicious fried as forcemeat balls and served with a roast leg of lamb.

Pork is usually very good value and I think you get the best out of it in a dish like Marinated Roast Pork by rubbing it with a seasoning mix to bring out its flavour and by taking great pains to achieve a really

M E N U

Marinated Roast Pork with Piquant Apple Sauce

Roast or Mashed Potatoes (no recipe)
Cabbage Braised with Caraway

———

Steamed Syrup Sponge with Lemon Curd Sauce

———

Potted Cheddar with Green Peppercorns and Cider

Variations

Tartlettes au Zeviche. Delicious little tarts with fish and a lemony mayonnaise.
Red Pepper and Lime Chartreuse with Fish Salad. A lovely fresh, fishy first course or a light summer lunch dish on its own.
Red Pepper and Lime Shapes with Curried Mayonnaise and Grapes. Another use for this jelly, this time turned out from individual cocottes and covered with a lightly curried grapey mayonnaise.

———

Guards of Honour. (page 23). One of the classic lamb dishes.
Leg of Lamb with Saffron and Almond Sauce (page 30). A traditional joint with an unusual sauce.
Gratin of Potato, Celeriac and Carrot (page 38). All-in-one vegetable which goes very well with a roast.

———

Hazelnut and Raspberry Tart (page 117). Lots of flavours.

crisp crackling which is half the joy of pork. A simple vegetable like Cabbage Braised with Caraway (caraway helps you to digest the pork), is easy to prepare and seems to get better with keeping warm. Don't be put off by its pedestrian sound because properly braised cabbage is a lovely dish. Alternatively, the Gratin of Potato, Celeriac and Carrot has the nice creamy texture that goes so well with a roast.

I wouldn't usually have a first course unless it was a particularly special occasion or unless I wanted to fill everyone up because I had rather a small roast! If I did, I might go for something fishy like Tartlettes au Zeviche. These use the same crisp cream cheese pastry shells that we've used in The Reliable Dinner or Supper Party but this time they are filled with a sharp, lemony-fishy mayonnaise and latticed with marinated fish. They are delightful, especially in summer, and provide a nice balance with what is to come, or you could just use the hot or cold Chicken Liver Tartlettes (page 15) themselves. Two others, the Red Pepper and Lime starters, are variations of each other; the Shapes, served with grapes and mayonnaise, are light and pretty but the Chartreuse, served with a white fish salad inside it would be a substantial enough main course in summer.

A classic Steamed Syrup Sponge, dressed up a bit with a Lemon Curd Sauce, is just perfect for a winter Sunday lunch, as is a hot Hazelnut and Raspberry Tart which in summer I would serve lukewarm or cold. Any fruit pudding or mousse, ice cream or sorbet would also make a fitting end to a lunch party and preferably, to my mind, served after the cheese. Sunday lunch usually includes cheese so get together a nice cheese board, including perhaps my Potted Cheddar recipe, which is also a useful standby for those moments when you can't get to the shops.

————— ‹ ✦ › —————

Marinated Roast Pork with Piquant Apple Sauce

A well flavoured and nicely roasted piece of pork, the crackling crisp and crunchy, is always a firm favourite for Sunday lunch. I always think pork is best as a lunch time meat, finding it perhaps a bit heavy for the evening. I like to marinate and flavour the pork before roasting to give it more taste and then to serve it with a piquant, sweet-sour apple sauce which sets it off well. For special occasions, loin is the best; the leg can sometimes be a little dry, but the less expensive blade or spare rib joint can often be delicious and excellent value.

Boned joints make for much easier carving, so get your butcher to bone it out or do it yourself if you wish. Allow about 6–8 oz (175–225 g) of boned meat per head or, for joints with the bone in, allow about 12 oz (350 g) per head.

I like to be generous for Sunday lunch and also have some cold meat for Monday, so I usually get a fair sized joint, finding this more economical in the end. Pork tends to be bred very lean these days but I try to choose a joint with some fat on it because this will render out and baste the joint whilst cooking, making the meat more tasty and succulent and stopping it from becoming dry.

for 6–8 people
5–6 lb (2.25–2.7 kg) loin, leg, blade bone or spare rib joint of pork
8–12 fl oz (225–350 ml) stock, vegetable water or wine and water for gravy
1–2 teaspoons potato flour (optional)
1 tablespoon mushroom ketchup (optional)

Marinade
1½ teaspoons sea salt
¼ teaspoon peppercorns
1 clove garlic
sprig sage, lemon thyme or thyme or ¼ teaspoon dried herb
½ bay leaf
2 tablespoons lemon juice
3 tablespoons olive oil
1 tablespoon calvados or brandy (optional)

Piquant Apple Sauce

1½ lb (675 g) cooking apples
1 oz (25 g) butter
1 onion
2–3 tablespoons sugar
2–3 tablespoons wine vinegar
3 cloves
freshly grated nutmeg
⅛ teaspoon ground allspice
½ in. (1 cm) grated fresh root ginger
1–2 teaspoons capers
pepper

Score the pork skin deeply into strips if this has not already been done by the butcher (a Stanley razor knife is good for this job).

Pound the peppercorns in a mortar until roughly crushed, then add the salt, garlic, herbs and crumbled bay leaf. Pound well together before dripping in the oil, lemon and calvados. Spread over the meat and rub it in well; even an hour or two of this marinade will give flavour to the meat but, for a large joint, up to three days is better but keep it in a cool place.

If necessary, tie the joint into a good shape and roast it, skin side up, without any fat (unless it is very lean) in a moderate oven (350°F/180°C/Gas 4), allowing 25–30 minutes to each pound. Half an hour from the end of the cooking time, baste the joint and turn the temperature up to hot (450°F/230°C/Gas 8) so the crackling really crispens. Add a little liquid to the pan if the juices look like burning, but let them get sticky and brown before adding liquid, for it is the browned meat juices that will give you the flavour and colour for your gravy.

Remove the meat to a serving dish and keep warm. Pour off excess fat and add stock, wine or vegetable water to the pan to make the gravy. Boil down, stirring in all the brown edges; correct seasoning and thicken, if you wish, with a little potato flour and water; if the colour is rather pale, add the mushroom ketchup. Correct seasoning, strain and serve it and the Piquant Apple Sauce separately.

Piquant Apple Sauce. Finely chop the onion and soften it in the butter. Peel, core and quarter the apples.

Use the 4 mm slicing disc. Slice the apples and add to the softened onion with the sugar, vinegar, cloves, nutmeg, allspice and ginger. Cover and cook gently until the apples have thrown some juice; then cook, uncovered, until the apples are completely tender and the mixture has become quite thick. Check the sugar and vinegar and adjust if necessary, stir in the capers and pepper and don't forget to fish out the cloves.

Use the double-bladed knife. Turn the apple into the Magimix and process until fairly smooth. Check the flavour, turn into a sauceboat or serving dish and keep warm.

The marinade being poured over the joint of pork and rubbed in to the surface

Cabbage Braised with Caraway

Caraway goes so well with cabbage and of course it is also good with pork as it helps the digestion of rich meats. This slowly braised dish of cabbage is a great favourite with us; it reheats beautifully or will keep warm almost indefinitely. The timings can vary considerably, depending on the maturity of the cabbage.

for 6–8 people
2–2½ lb (900 g–1.5 kg) white cabbage
2–3 oz (50–75 g) butter
½ teaspoon caraway seeds
salt and pepper

Use the standard or 4 mm slicing disc. Cut the cabbage to fit the feed tube, discard the core and slice. Throw the cabbage into a large pan of boiling, salted water and blanch for 2–5 minutes; drain and refresh under the cold tap, then squeeze well to expel moisture.

Heat the butter in a large casserole until sizzling, then add the cabbage, seasoning and caraway seeds. Toss well in the butter then press down, cover closely and cook in a slow oven (300°F/150°C/Gas 2) for ¾ –2 hours until very tender. If the juices have not all disappeared, remove the lid and boil fast until the cabbage is virtually dry. Correct seasoning and serve or it can be kept warm or reheated.

Cutting the cabbage into wedges to fit into the feed tube

Steamed Syrup Sponge with Lemon Curd Sauce

Wafer thin slices of thin-skinned lemon are placed around the bowl with generous quantities of syrup. After long steaming, they give a wonderful fresh flavour to this feather light sponge, served with a Lemon Curd Sauce which you can flavour with brandy if you like. Quick to prepare, it can then be forgotten while it steams for a couple of hours. Make this pudding by the Magimix all-in-one method, beating all the ingredients together, but make sure you really have the butter as soft as it can be without melting; so soft it plops off the spoon with a tiny shake.

for 6–8 people
3 eggs
weight of the eggs in very soft butter, in castor sugar
    and in self raising flour
¼ teaspoon salt
grated rind 1 lemon
4 tablespoons milk
1 thin-skinned lemon
3–4 tablespoons golden syrup

Lemon Curd Sauce
4 oz (100 g) sugar
5 fl oz (150 ml) cold water
1½ teaspoons cornflour
1 egg
grated rind and juice 1 lemon
2–3 oz (50–75 g) butter
2–3 tablespoons brandy (optional)

Prepare the bowl first and set your pan of water to boil. Generously butter a 2½ pint (1.5 l) pudding basin. Carefully spoon golden syrup around the bottom and sides of the bowl. Cut wafer thin slices from the thin-skinned lemon (one with thick white pith can be too bitter) and decorate all over the inside of the bowl, pressing them into the syrup.
Use the double-bladed knife. Place the soft butter, sugar, salt, grated lemon rind, eggs, self raising flour and milk into the bowl and process for 6–8 seconds. Stop and scrape the mixture down, then process again for no more than 2–4 seconds until completely mixed. Over processing is the most likely reason for a less than perfect sponge.

Turn the mixture into the prepared pudding basin, cover with a butter paper and layer of tinfoil, carefully crimped round the edges. Stand the bowl, either in a steamer over boiling water, or in a large pan with either a couple of skewers, a trivet or folded cloth to keep the bowl off the bottom of the pan; the water should come half way up the outside of the bowl. Boil for 2 hours, adding more boiling water as necessary.

To Serve. Remove the bowl from the saucepan or steamer, uncover and, very carefully, run a flexible knife round the inside of the bowl. Turn out the pudding and serve with Lemon Curd Sauce.

Lemon Curd Sauce. Place the sugar, water and grated lemon rind in a saucepan and bring to the boil, stirring to dissolve the sugar. Mix the cornflour with a little cold water and add to the syrup; bring to the boil and boil for about 1 minute until clear.

Use the double-bladed knife. Break the egg into the Magimix bowl and process for 10–15 seconds; then pour the boiling syrup down the feed tube while the engine is running. Drop in the butter and add the lemon juice and brandy (if used). Return the sauce to the pan and heat gently (do not boil or the egg will curdle) until the sauce thickens. Keep warm and serve with the Steamed Syrup Sponge.

Spreading the golden syrup over the sides of the pudding bowl

Wafer thin slices being cut from a thin skinned lemon

Arranging the slices inside the bowl

When turning the sponge mixture into the bowl, be very careful not to dislodge the lemon slices

The pudding turned out and looking pretty on a serving dish

Potted Cheddar with Green Peppercorns and Cider

Not living near a good cheese shop, I often find I am caught without any decent cheese. This potted cheddar, which can be made from cheese that has been in the freezer, has often come to my rescue. It's really nicest when freshly made and still soft and creamy; after refrigeration it goes firmer and more crumbly but the flavour is still good.

1 lb (450 g) approx.
12 oz (350 g) cheddar cheese
3 oz (75 g) soft butter
6–8 tablespoons cider
1–1½ teaspoons green peppercorns
small handful parsley heads or celery leaves

Use the fine grating disc. Grate the cheese and set aside.
Change to the double-bladed knife. Warm the cider a little so it will be more easily absorbed by the cheese. Cream the butter in the Magimix until really soft, then add the grated cheese, the green peppercorns and the parsley or celery leaves. Process to a cream, gradually adding the warmed cider until you have a soft creamy mixture; season only if necessary. Turn out and mound up on a cheese board and decorate with herbs or watercress or pack into a pot to serve.

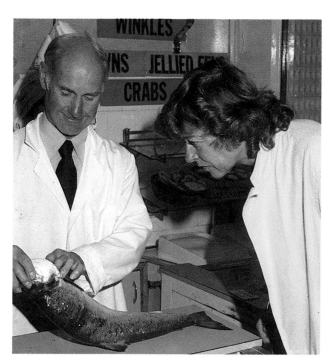

Nicola examines a salmon with her fishmonger

The colourful ingredients for the Potted Cheddar with Green Peppercorns and Cider

Tartlettes au Zeviche

Wafers of fine raw fish, marinated in lime or lemon juice, are used to decorate little cream cheese pastry shells, filled with a light mayonnaise. Salmon gives the greatest effect, the colour contrasting beautifully with the pale mayonnaise and tasting really good. When I use a white fish, I sprinkle the tartlettes with tiny dice of red pepper or tiny red currants and sprigs of fresh coriander to provide a lovely contrast.

for 6–8 people
10–12 oz (275–350 g) very fresh salmon, turbot, cod or haddock fillet
3–4 limes or 2–3 lemons
salt and pepper

Zeviche Mayonnaise
2 egg yolks
¾ teaspoon dijon mustard
10–12 fl oz (300–350 ml) sunflower or light oil
2–4 tablespoons liquid from the marinated fish
salt and pepper
fresh coriander or parsley to decorate
tiny dice of red pepper or a few red currants to decorate (optional)
6–8 cream cheese pastry tartlettes (page 15)

Skin the fish and remove any bones; then slice lengthways into wafer slices or strips. Lay the fish in a bowl, season with salt and pepper and cover with lime or lemon juice. Marinate for 6–24 hours until opaque and looking like cooked fish.

Creamed Cheese Pastry Tartlettes. Make and cook as on page 15 but continue to bake for 10 minutes or so until the pastry is light golden brown and completely cooked. Then cool on a rack and store in an airtight tin until ready to serve.

Zeviche Mayonnaise. *Use the double-bladed knife.* Place the egg yolks in the Magimix bowl and add salt, pepper, mustard and 1 tablespoon of liquid from the marinating fish. Process for 15–20 seconds, then gradually add the oil in a fine thread to make a thick mayonnaise; add additional spoonfuls of fish marinating liquid until the mayonnaise is quite sharp and limey but still of spreading consistency.

To Assemble. Drain the fish well in a sieve. Fill the tartlettes with a layer of mayonnaise then arrange the well drained fish in an attractive pattern on the mayonnaise. Decorate with red currants or tiny dice or red pepper and sprigs of fresh coriander or parsley, or just finely chopped parsley. Serve preferably within an hour or so of assembling.

With the Magimix working the oil for the Zeviche Mayonnaise is carefully poured in through the feed tube

Mayonnaise of a spreading consistency is used for this dish

The Tartlettes can be decorated to look really sensational

Red Pepper and Lime Chartreuse with Fish Salad

This red pepper and lime jelly, set in a ring mould and filled with a lovely, clean tasting white fish salad makes a fresh starter or a nice light summer lunch dish for fewer people. I must say I love these clean tastes which are neither heavy nor cloying on the palate.

I also serve little individual moulds of the Red Pepper Chartreuse, with a lightly curried mayonnaise with grapes, which makes another delicious and unusual starter. Sometimes I fill the ring of Red Pepper Chartreuse with a crispy green bean salad, scattered with a few browned almonds or pinenuts. To get the proper flavour, one really must grill the peppers until the skin is black all over and the peppers have softened; this is a task I used to find impossible and time consuming, until I suddenly realised you just toss the red peppers (buy the smoothest ones you can find) under the grill or onto the naked gas flame and get on with something else, turning them from time to time until the skins really are crisp and black all over. Then you give them a really good rub under cold running water until all the skin comes off. Once roasted, you can pop them in a sealed plastic bag and leave them to cool; the skins are then supposed to rub off more easily but I can't say I have found it much of an improvement and it means you have to wait before continuing with the dish.

for 6–8 people
Red Pepper and Lime Chartreuse
1½ lb (675 g) red peppers
1½ tablespoons gelatine
4 tablespoons boiling water
3 spring onions
1 small clove garlic
3–4 leaves fresh or ¼ teaspoon dried basil or
    marjoram
rind and juice of 1 – 2 limes or 1 lemon (or to taste if
    limes are large)
1¼ pints (750 ml) chicken stock
salt and pepper

To Garnish
1 bunch watercress

Fish Salad
1½ lb (675 g) haddock or cod fillet
1 tablespoon salt
2–3 slices lime or lemon

Mayonnaise Dressing
2 egg yolks
8 fl oz (250 ml) mixed olive and light oil (sunflower)
1–2 limes or 1 lemon
½ clove garlic
5 fl oz (150 ml) plain yoghurt
1 teaspoon dijon mustard
chopped chives
salt and pepper

Lay the peppers under a hot grill or put them directly over the gas flame and keep turning them until the skins blacken all over and the peppers are soft. Then rinse and rub off the blackened skins under the cold tap and pat dry on kitchen paper. Remove the stalk and de-seed the peppers, retaining all the juice that runs out.

Use the double-bladed knife. Place the gelatine in the Magimix, pour in the boiling water and process until the gelatine has dissolved. Add in the peppers, spring onions, garlic and herbs and process to a purée before adding the grated rind and juice of the limes and half the chicken stock. Season and process, then pour through a sieve onto the remaining chicken stock and mix together before turning into a lightly oiled 2 pints (1.2 l) ring mould. Leave to set.

Fish Salad. Bring a pan of water to the boil and add the salt and lime or lemon slices. Add the fish fillet, cover and remove from the heat; leave to stand in a warm place for 10 minutes, then, still with closed pan, set aside until cold. Remove the skin and bones and flake the fish into large chunks.

Mayonnaise Dressing. *Use the double-bladed knife.* Place the 2 yolks, salt, pepper, mustard and crushed garlic in the Magimix bowl with some grated lime rind and a little juice. Process for about 10 seconds then trickle in the oil to make a stiff mayonnaise (see Magimix Mayonnaise page 101). Correct seasoning, add plenty of lime juice, combine with the yoghurt and chives and fold in the flaked fish.

To Assemble. Run the tip of a knife round the two rims of the Pepper Chartreuse. Dip the mould into warm water, dry then turn out onto a serving dish. Pile the fish in the centre, scissor over some chives and surround with sprigs of watercress.

Variation

Red Pepper and Lime Shapes with Curried Mayonnaise and Grapes.

Make the Red Pepper and Lime Chartreuse above but, instead of turning it into a ring mould, turn into lightly oiled 4 fl oz (100 ml) moulds or cocotte dishes and leave to set. Turn out onto individual plates and spoon over some Curried Mayonnaise and Grapes.

Curried Mayonnaise and Grapes. Make up the basic Mayonnaise as in the white fish salad but make it with 1 egg rather than 2 yolks and add, with the egg, 1 teaspoon curry paste or powder (Mild Madras) and 1 teaspoon of chopped Mild Lime Pickle (it's a wonderful flavour; I often pop a tiny bit into dressings and sauces to give them a little extra something). Once made, add grated lime rind and juice to taste and fold in 8 oz (225 g) halved and de-pipped white grapes (the texture of the dish is much better if you can bear to skin them first; ½–1 minute in boiling water then plunged into cold water). Correct seasoning and, if necessary, thin with a little yoghurt, cream or milk. Spoon over the turned out shapes when serving.

The Red Pepper and Lime Chartreuse with Fish Salad is not too difficult to make and your guests will be thrilled with its sensational colours

An Informal Supper Party

MENU

Starters

Celeriac Remoulade

Prawn Stuffed Eggs

Sardine and Spinach Pâté

Beetroot and Onion Salad

Brown Soda Scone

Main Courses

Home Made Pasta Flavoured with Basil

Salsa di Funghi

Spinach Roulade with Creamed Haddock Filling

Spicy Mince and Green Peppercorn Pie

Vegetables

Salad with Italian Dressing

Puddings

Chocolate Orange Mousse

Apple Streusel with Grand Marnier and Almond Cream

Mango Ice Cream

Isn't informality part of our age? Aren't the last minute visitors, the casual invitations, the relaxed occasion really our most usual form of entertaining? The scene is the kitchen and the style is eclectic; anything goes, as long as it is good, preferably inexpensive, quick to prepare and you have the ingredients. In this chapter I have not really prepared a menu so much as suggested several ideas, leaving your purse and inclination to dictate the choice.

The first course can grow like Topsy should your party suddenly get bigger. The Prawn Stuffed Eggs, Celeriac Remoulade (which by the way will keep for several weeks or even months, well covered in the fridge, and is an extremely useful standby) or Spinach and Sardine Pâté are all good on their own; but should you want an hors d'oeuvre effect for larger numbers, prepare two or all three of these, add black olives and a sliced beetroot and onion salad (or any other bright vegetable salad) for depth and colour and you are away.

Brown Soda Scone honestly takes less time to make in the Magimix than it takes to read the recipe. I pat it out in a round on a baking sheet then, with twenty minutes in a hot oven it's ready to eat and is really at its best when eaten warm. So breakfast, lunch, tea or supper time, it's a true and trusty friend and a great standby should you ever run out of bread.

I did not know where to stop with main courses because so many useful dishes sprang to mind. Yet again, the Magimix proves itself an invaluable ally in helping one to provide inexpensive, quick and delicious dishes.

For the instant occasion when the cupboard is bare, Home Made Pasta Flavoured with Basil is a great standby. I promise you, it can be hot on the plate within half an hour of walking into the kitchen

though, admittedly, this means rolling it with a pasta machine and having the experience of making pasta once or twice before. I serve it with just butter and parmesan, grated with the parmesan grater from the slab in the bottom of my fridge. When time is even shorter, I use packet pasta and toss it with chopped fresh basil, which has been creamed with butter and is kept as a block in the freezer. When you have mushrooms, you can serve home-made or packet pasta with the excellent Salsa di Funghi. It can be made in about the time it takes packet pasta to cook.

The Spinach Roulade is in a different category; it takes a little longer to make, but from the simple ingredients of spinach, eggs and a little smoked fish, you have an elegant dish which would do equally well for a much grander party. It's really an all-in-one dish and needs nothing with it, though a few new potatoes and a salad would be nice. This pretty green and gold Swiss roll is served hot though we think it's also rather good cold. The Spicy Mince and Green Peppercorn Pie is a nice mince variation which, when topped with our Magimix Rough Puff Pastry, becomes a really good savoury pie.

I'm only including one vegetable, a Salad with Italian Dressing which would go well with any of the main courses.

For afters, there is the almost instant Chocolate Orange Mousse or the Mango Ice Cream which only requires a tin of mangoes (unless you can find a fresh mango or two), time for it to freeze – and a Magimix to whisk it to a smooth creamy consistency. Though slightly more trouble the homely Apple Streusel adds a spicy continental touch.

Quick preparation is what this chapter is all about because that is what most of us need rather more often than something more special.

———————— ✦ ————————

Celeriac Remoulade

I love this typically french salad of shredded celeriac in a mustardy mayonnaise. It is well worth making an extra bowl because, well covered in the fridge, it will keep for months. It is a most useful addition to a mixed hors d'oeuvre or it can be served on its own with fresh bread or Brown Soda Scone.

for 6–8 people
2 roots celeriac, approx. 1 lb (450 g) each
1 lemon
plenty of salt

Dressing
½ pint (300 ml) Magimix Mayonnaise (page 101)
4–5 tablespoons dijon mustard
2–3 tablespoons wine vinegar
salt and pepper

Use the citrus press. Squeeze the lemon into the Magimix bowl.
Change to the julienne or coarse grating disc. Cut the celeriac into slices no thicker than the width of the Magimix feed tube, then peel off the skin. Cut into pieces and grate into the lemon juice in the Magimix bowl. Toss the celeriac quickly in the lemon juice to prevent discolouration and season heavily with salt. Leave for ½–1 hour for the salt to draw out moisture; then rinse under the cold tap, drain and squeeze out as much liquid as you can, using your hands.

Mix the mustard and vinegar into the Magimix Mayonnaise, then stir in the drained celeriac. Keep for several hours or overnight before using.

The filling for the Prawn Stuffed Eggs processed and ready for use

For a special occasion a dish of Prawn Stuffed Eggs can be decorated with whole unshelled prawns

Prawn Stuffed Eggs

So simple yet so good and I find everyone loves this recipe. It can easily be made with prawns from the freezer; or you can make it into something both attractive and special with a few fresh, unshelled prawns as garnish. These eggs are also good served on sliced, dressed tomatoes which makes it into a good summer lunch dish if you increase the quantities.

If you haven't any prawns, the stuffing is still good and the Magimix makes such a lovely smooth filling.

for 6–8 people
6–8 eggs
2 oz (50 g) soft butter
1–1½ teaspoons anchovy essence
3–4 oz (75–100 g) shelled prawns
1–2 tablespoons cream or milk if necessary
good pinch mace
a little cayenne pepper
salt if necessary
unshelled prawns to garnish (optional)

Boil the eggs for 10 minutes then plunge into cold water to stop them cooking and to prevent a blue ring forming round the yolk. Peel and halve the eggs lengthways, remove the yolks and set the whites aside.
Use the double-bladed knife. Cream the butter then add in the egg yolks, anchovy, mace and cayenne. Process again until very smooth, then add in most of the prawns (keeping back 6–8 for decoration) and process to chop the prawns roughly. Correct seasoning and thin, if necessary, with a little cream or milk. Pile into the halves of egg whites and decorate with the reserved prawns. Serve with a garnish of unshelled prawns if you wish.

Sardine and Spinach Pâté

A fresh green pâté, quickly made with cooked spinach and a couple of tins of sardines. It is nice as a starter, as part of a mixed hors d'oeuvre, as a simple lunch dish or for filling rolls for a picnic.

for 6–8 people
6 oz (175 g) cooked spinach, quite well squeezed
2 tins sardines
1 shallot or piece of spring onion
juice ½ lemon or to taste
freshly grated nutmeg
salt and pepper

Use the double-bladed knife. Drain the sardines, keeping the oil. Process the spinach and shallot or onion until well chopped and then add in the sardines, the grated nutmeg, lemon juice and seasoning. Process until smooth and add in some of the reserved sardine oil if the mixture is too thick; correct seasoning and pack into a pot. Serve with hot toast, rolls or french bread.

Spreading Sardine and Spinach Pâté onto a wedge of fresh Brown Soda Scone

Beetroot and Onion Salad

Sliced beetroot with sweet raw onion in a dill dressing makes a nice simple vegetable first course. It can also be used as a component of a mixed hors d'oeuvre or as a salad. It's surprising how much vinegar and sugar beetroot needs to get it just right. The little bit of raw onion (sweet spanish or the mild red-skinned ones are the nicest but use finely chopped shallot, onion or spring onion if necessary) makes all the difference to the flavour.

for 6–8 people
2 lb (900 g) cooked beetroot
3–4 oz (75–100 g) sweet spanish onion
1 tablespoon castor sugar
3–4 tablespoons wine vinegar
5–6 tablespoons good olive oil
sprig or two of fresh or ¼ teaspoon dried dill
salt and very coarsely ground black pepper

Use the 4 mm slicing disc. Slice the beetroot with light pressure on the plunger and lay in a wide dish.
Change to the standard slicing disc. Slice the onion finely and scatter over the beetroot.
Change to the double-bladed knife. Put all the remaining ingredients, including a sprig of dill, into the Magimix and process to chop the dill and mix the dressing. Pour over the beetroot and decorate with additional sprigs of dill.

Brown Soda Scone

Based on an old Scottish recipe from my great-great-grandmother, this is so quick to make that you can be eating it within half an hour of thinking about it; don't blame me if you get indigestion from eating it too hot! It's nicest served freshly made and just warm and is very good for breakfast or tea. Cooked all-in-one, there is no messing about rolling and cutting the mixture, though of course you can make it into conventional scones if you wish.

1 scone loaf
12 oz (350 g) mixed wholemeal and white flour (half and half or two thirds to one third as you like)
¾ teaspoon bicarbonate of soda
1½ teaspoons cream of tartar
½ pint (300 ml) half and half yoghurt and milk mixed
¾ teaspoon salt

Use the double-bladed knife. Place the flours in the Magimix bowl with the bicarbonate of soda, cream of tartar and salt. Process to mix thoroughly then add the yoghurt and milk mixture through the feed tube to make a soft but not too sticky dough. Do not over-process because scone mixes become tough if over-worked. Turn out onto a floured baking sheet and pat into an 8 in. (20 cm) disc. Cut the top across and across four times to make eight segments, cutting only ½ in. (1 cm) deep. Then cook the loaf in a hot oven (425°F/220°C/Gas 7) for about 20 minutes until well risen and brown. Cool on a rack and serve with pâtés, soups or starters or for breakfast or tea.

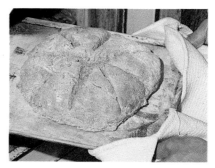

The texture of the dough for the Brown Soda Scone should be soft, but not sticky. Before baking cut across the scone to mark the segments. Cook the scone for about 20 minutes until well risen and brown

Home Made Pasta Flavoured with Basil

Home made pasta is so light and delicious that it knocks any bought pasta into a cocked hat. Your Magimix does all the tedious kneading for you, leaving you only the rolling to do, child's play with a pasta machine and not so difficult without.

for 6–8 people
1 lb (450 g) strong bread flour
4 large eggs
1 tablespoon dried basil
1 tablespoon olive oil
1 teaspoon salt

Use the double-bladed knife. Place the eggs, basil and oil in the Magimix bowl, add the flour and salt and process for about 1 minute. The mixture should stay in polystyrene-like granules and not draw into one lump until the end. Add more flour if it forms a sticky lump or drip in a tiny bit of water if it won't draw together. Press the dough into one lump (you always want to work with it as dry as possible) and divide into 7–8 pieces; if rolling out by hand, divide into 2 or 3 bits. Keep the bits you are not rolling in a plastic bag. Pass each piece of dough through the pasta machine; if it is not very smooth, fold and pass it through several times, starting at the widest setting and getting progressively thinner to about the one from finest setting. Keep the pasta well floured at all times. Then cut the pasta into ribbon noodles, sprinkle with flour (or a mixture of flour and fine polenta (maize meal) which is even better) and shake out into little piles on a floured tray; leave to dry for about ½–2 hours or you can cook it immediately.

By hand, roll each bit of pasta until very thin and about 15 × 15 in. (38 × 38 cm); the pasta should be like a piece of chamois leather and thin enough to see the grain of the table through. Flour well, roll up loosely and cut across into ribbons of whatever width you like. The pasta can be frozen when made, cut and rested. Pack loosely into plastic bags and freeze.
To Cook. Toss into plenty of salted boiling water, about 8–12 pints (4.5–6.7 l) with 1–2 tablespoons of added oil and cook for 3–5 minutes until al dente; allow a few moments longer from frozen. Drain and use as desired.

Adding the dried basil to the pasta ingredients in the Magimix bowl

The processed pasta dough

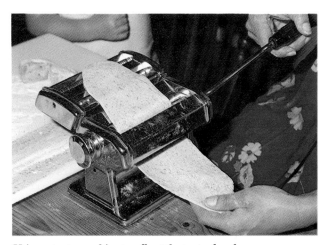

Using a pasta machine to roll out the pasta dough

Salsa di Funghi

A simpler, quicker to make sauce is hard to imagine. It really is excellent and goes very well with the basil pasta.

for 6–8 people
3 tablespoons olive oil
2 oz (50 g) butter
1 large onion
good big handful parsley heads
2–3 cloves garlic
½ oz (12 g) plain flour
¾–1 lb (350–450 g) very fresh button mushrooms
salt and pepper

To Toss with the Pasta
1 oz (25 g) butter
2–3 tablespoons cream
salt and pepper

To Hand Separately
freshly grated parmesan

Use the double-bladed knife. Roughly chop the onion in the Magimix with the on/off technique and turn into the butter and oil, heated in a flameproof casserole. Add the parsley and garlic to the bowl and chop finely; add to the casserole and fry until very light golden; sprinkle over the flour and cook for a minute or so.
Change to the standard slicing disc. Pack the tube carefully with the washed mushrooms and slice with firm pressure. Add the mushrooms to the casserole, season and simmer, covered, until the mushrooms are just cooked. They should produce enough liquid to make a sauce but add a little stock or water if it's too thick. Boil fast, uncovered, if the sauce is too liquid.
To Serve. Heat a little butter and 2–3 tablespoons cream in a wide serving dish. Turn the cooked and drained pasta into this dish and season and toss it. Add the Salsa di Funghi and toss again so each strand of pasta is coated in rich sauce. Hand freshly grated parmesan separately.

Spinach Roulade with Creamed Haddock Filling

The gold and green layers of this roulade are pretty and it's good hot or cold. It's just right for informal entertaining; not too grand, made from simple ingredients but interesting and delicious.

for 6–8 people
2 lb (900 g) fresh or 1¼ lb (550 g) frozen spinach
3–4 slices stale bread
1 onion
3½ oz (85 g) butter
3 oz (75 g) plain flour
1 pint (600 ml) milk
6 eggs
salt, pepper and nutmeg

Creamed Haddock Filling
the remaining half of the white sauce kept back from
    making the spinach roulade
12 oz (350 g) smoked haddock fillet
3 oz (75 g) cheddar cheese
a little cream or milk
salt and pepper

Use the double-bladed knife. Process the torn up crustless bread to fine breadcrumbs and dry off in a slow oven.
   Line a 10 × 18 in. (25 × 45 cm) roasting or baking tin with heavily buttered Bakewell paper or tinfoil and sprinkle with half the dried breadcrumbs.
   Throw the washed and picked over spinach into plenty of boiling, salted water in a non-aluminium pan (aluminium reacts with spinach to give that tooth-edgy flavour). Boil until just tender, drain in a colander and refresh under the cold tap. Squeeze out the spinach by handfuls until dry. Set aside.
Use the double-bladed knife. Place the roughly cut up onion in the Magimix bowl and finely chop with the on/off technique; add to half an ounce of the butter, melted, and fry until golden. Add it to the spinach.
   Chop up and melt the remaining 3 oz (75 g) of butter in a saucepan; add the flour and cook stirring all the time over moderate heat for 2–3 minutes. Draw off the stove and, when sizzling ceases, add the milk. Bring to the boil, whisking hard, and simmer for 1–2 minutes.
Use the double-bladed knife. Place the spinach and onion in the Magimix and chop (not too fine); add

half the white sauce and season with salt, pepper and nutmeg. Process and drop the egg yolks down the feed tube one at a time. Whisk the egg whites in a large bowl until just holding a peak and then carefully fold in the spinach mixture; pour it carefully down the side of the bowl so it does not squash the air out of the egg whites. Turn the mixture into the prepared tin, spread smoothly to an even thickness and bake in a moderately hot oven (375°F/190°C/Gas 5) for 12–18 minutes until the middle feels springy and the edges are shrinking slightly.

Have another sheet of Bakewell paper or greased tinfoil sprinkled with the remaining dried breadcrumbs on a baking sheet. Loosen the roulade edges and invert onto the prepared sheet (it will keep in a very slow oven for half an hour or so). When ready to serve, peel off the top sheet, spread the roulade with the prepared filling and roll up like a swiss roll, using the Bakewell or tinfoil to aid you. Roll onto a serving dish and serve at once.

Creamed Haddock Filling. *Use the fine grating disc.* Grate the cheese. Skin and cube the smoked haddock and add it to the remaining sauce in the saucepan. Cook gently, turning carefully and thinning with a little cream or milk if necessary, until the fish is cooked and the mixture is of a good filling consistency (not too thin). Add the grated cheese and then season with pepper, but salt only if necessary. Keep the filling warm over hot water until ready to use.

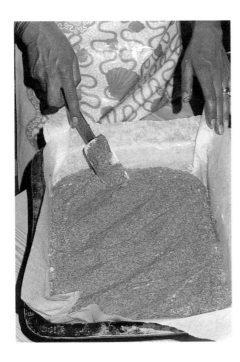

The Spinach Roulade being made, rolled and finally cut into colourful slices

Spicy Mince and Green Peppercorn Pie

I prefer to buy meat and chop it myself in the Magimix. You then know what you are getting and, because the meat is chopped rather than minced, it remains more succulent and juicy. You can serve the Spicy Mince on its own or cover it with our very quickly made Rough Puff Pastry to make it into a pie. A pie always has more style than simple mince, don't you think?

for 6–8 people
2 lb (900 g) stewing or braising beef (clod or chuck)
3 onions
2 oz (50 g) fat
1 oz (25 g) flour
1½–2 teaspoons curry powder
1½ teaspoons Worcester sauce
1 tablespoon chutney
½–1 teaspoon green peppercorns
1 pint (600 ml) stock or 1 beef stock cube (Knorr) and water

Rough Puff Pastry
8 oz (225 g) plain flour
2 oz (50 g) firm chilled butter
2 oz (50 g) chilled lard
6–7 tablespoons iced water
½ teaspoon salt
egg yolk

Rough Puff Pastry. Cut the butter and lard into little fingernail sized cubes and chill well; a few moments in the freezer is a good idea.
Use the double-bladed knife. Place the flour and salt in the Magimix bowl and process for several seconds to 'sift'; add the chilled butter and lard cubes. Have the measured water ready. Switch on and pour the water down the tube and switch off the moment the pastry draws together and while the fats are still in pea-sized bits. Turn onto a floured board, knead briefly together and roll to a roughly 9 × 5 in. (24 × 13 cm) rectangle. Brush off excess flour and turn the top third down and the bottom third up; press the edges together, turn a quarter turn clockwise and roll and fold once more. Pop in a plastic bag to rest in the fridge for ½–2 hours.

Spicy Mince and Green Peppercorns. *Use the double-bladed knife.* Cut the onions roughly into the Magimix bowl, chop with the on/off technique and add to the hot fat in a frying pan or casserole; fry the onions to a good brown colour and remove. Trim the meat of gristle and cut into cubes. (You can chill the meat in the freezer, until firm but still taking a thumb-nail indentation, for easy mincing).

Switch on the Magimix and drop half the meat down the tube; process until minced, remove then chop the remaining meat. If you are using one of the bigger machines you can, of course, chop all the meat at one time. Fry the meat in hot fat until brown, best done in several batches, adding more fat if necessary; return all to the pan, sprinkle over the flour and cook for several minutes before stirring in all the flavourings and the stock or cube and water. Bring to the boil, stirring, and either cover and cook or turn into a casserole and cook for about 15–30 minutes until tender and a thick rich mixture. Turn the mince into a 2 pint (1.2 l) pie dish with pie funnel in place and leave until cold. Roll the pastry to ⅛ in. (3 mm) thickness and cut a ½ in. (1.5 cm) strip from all round the edge. Damp the rim of the pie dish with cold water and set the strip in place all round. Now moisten the strip of pastry and carefully cover the pie with remaining pastry; seal the edges with a fork, decorate and make a small hole for steam to escape; brush with egg wash and cook in a hot oven (425°F/220°C/Gas 7) until a good brown; turn down to moderately hot (375°F/190°C/Gas 5) and continue to bake for about 1 hour, covering lightly with tinfoil when brown enough, to ensure the pastry is cooked right through.

Chocolate Mousse is always a favourite and the orange adds that extra something

Chocolate Orange Mousse

When time is short you will bless this pudding because it really is almost instant. We use the cheating method of melting gelatine and chocolate (but hold your hat on if the chocolate is cold for it can rattle round the bowl a bit before it melts; if I have time, I usually leave it somewhere to soften a little first).

Chocolate and orange is such a wonderful combination of flavours anyway, but try serving this with a fluffy heap of Grand Marnier and Almond Cream – I think you will like it. The Almond Shortbread Fingers (page 17) also go well with it.

for 6–8 people
4½ oz (112 g) good dark chocolate like Bournville, Terry's or Menier
1 tablespoon gelatine
8 fl oz (225 ml) milk
3 oz (75 g) castor sugar
½ teaspoon powdered coffee
grated rind of 1 orange
5 separated eggs
8 fl oz (225 ml) double or whipping cream
1–2 Grand Marnier (optional)

Have all the ingredients ready.
Use the double-bladed knife. Place gelatine, coffee and grated orange rind in the Magimix bowl. Heat milk to boiling point. Switch on and pour the milk down the tube, then process for 5 seconds for the gelatine to melt before dropping in the egg yolks, followed by the sugar. To stop the mixture splattering, cover the feed tube with your hand; then carefully post the chocolate, cube by cube, between your thumb and finger down the feed tube. The machine will jump as the chocolate hits the blades but it very quickly melts. Process until absolutely smooth then add the cream and, if used, the Grand Marnier. Process for a further 10–15 seconds only and switch off. Cool for 10–15 minutes or until thickening slightly. Whip the egg whites until just holding a peak then fold in the chocolate mixture and turn into a 2 pint (1.2 l) soufflé dish.

Salad with Italian Dressing

I love this tasty dressing which can be used with crisp lettuce, chinese leaves or any mixed salad ingredients. I always try to use one of those really good green olive oils, preferably a first pressing virgin tuscan oil, for this dressing as it really does give it the right flavour.

for 6–8 people
head of crisp lettuce or chinese leaves
tomatoes
cucumber
firm button mushrooms
florence fennel   } any of these
crisp baby courgettes   that are available
celery
radicchio
a few black olives (optional)

Dressing
1 clove garlic
3–4 anchovy fillets
1 teaspoon capers
small handful of fresh parsley
several leaves of fresh or pinch dried tarragon or basil
juice of ½–1 lemon
4–5 fl oz (100–150 ml) best olive oil
pepper

Use the double-bladed knife. Place the peeled clove of garlic, the anchovies, capers, parsley and tarragon or basil in the Magimix with a little pepper; the anchovies should provide enough salt. Process and add the lemon and oil (the parsley will chop quickly once liquid has been added), stopping to stir down once so all gets evenly chopped.

Place the washed and crisped lettuce in a salad bowl and arrange the other vegetables attractively on top.
Change to standard slicing disc. Slice the cucumber, button mushrooms, fennel and courgettes in the Magimix. By hand, quarter the tomatoes, chop the celery and pluck the radicchio to pieces. Scatter with olives, if used, and I sometimes use borage flowers, marigold petals or nasturtium flowers to add more colour to the salad. Pour over the dressing and toss only when ready to serve.

Apple Streusel

This German sponge pudding, layered with sliced apple and topped with spicy crumbs, makes an unusual hot pudding, especially when served with Grand Marnier and Almond Cream. It can also be served cold, cut into squares, as a cake. It was always one of our favourites bought from our German baker but I used to find it rather a fiddle to make myself. Now the Magimix can make the sponge, slice the apples and whizz up the crumble all in a flash and it's almost too easy. Make this sponge mixture by the Magimix all-in-one method, beating together all the ingredients, but making sure the butter is really soft, so soft it is practically but not quite melting.

for 6–8 people
1½ lb (675) cooking apples
5 oz (125 g) very soft butter
5 oz (125 g) castor sugar
2 large eggs
grated rind ½ lemon
8 oz (225 g) S.R. flour
3–4 tablespoons milk
pinch salt

Streusel Topping
2 oz (50 g) self raising flour
1½ oz (35 g) firm butter
1 oz (25 g) soft brown or demerara sugar
¼–½ teaspoon mixed spice
grated rind ½ lemon
1–2 tablespoons flaked or ground almonds
2–3 drops vanilla essence

First place the eggs in a bowl of warm water to warm a little so they will be absorbed by the butter and sugar more easily. Then butter a 8 × 12 in. (20 × 30 cm) shallow ovenproof dish or roasting tin.
Use the double-bladed knife. Place the very soft butter, sugar, eggs, grated lemon rind, self raising flour, milk and salt in the bowl and process for 6–8 seconds. Scrape the mixture down from the sides and process for a further 2–4 seconds only, until completely mixed. Spread the mixture into the prepared dish.
Use the 4 mm slicing disc. Peel, core and quarter the apples. Pack the feed tube carefully with apple quarters on their sides, and slice the apples with firm pressure. Arrange the slices in over-lapping rows on top of the sponge mixture.

Change to the double-bladed knife. Place the flour, diced butter, sugar, spice, grated lemon rind, vanilla essence and almonds in the Magimix bowl and process until it forms large crumbs. Scatter the streusel topping over the apple slices and cook in a moderate oven (350°F/180°C/Gas 4) for about 35–45 minutes until cooked and brown on top. Cut into squares or slices and serve hot, warm or cold, with Grand Marnier and Almond Cream if you wish.

———————— : ————————

Grand Marnier and Almond Cream

A quick, delicious and very useful cream to whisk up in a second to accompany Apple Streusel or steamed puddings, pancakes, fruit pies or mousses; in fact, it's lovely with any pudding where thick cream with a divine flavour won't go amiss.

a bowlful
6–8 fl oz (175–225 ml) whipping cream
2 tablespoons icing sugar
¼ teaspoon almond essence
1–1½ tablespoons Grand Marnier or other orange
  flavoured liqueur

Use the double-bladed knife. Place all the ingredients in the Magimix bowl and process for about 20 seconds until thick; do not over-process or you could turn the cream to butter. Spoon into a bowl and serve.

Testing the sugar syrup for the 'short thread' stage

Mango Ice Cream

Mangoes give a marvellous flavour and texture to an ice cream. This is a really wonderful quick recipe that makes a very smooth ice cream.

for 4–6 people
15 oz (425 g) tin mangoes
4 oz (100 g) castor sugar
1 egg
2 egg yolks
8 fl oz (225 ml) whipping cream
1 lemon or to taste

Strain the juice from the tin of mangoes which should give you about 6 fl oz (175 ml) of syrup. Place the syrup and sugar in a small saucepan and stir to dissolve the sugar; then boil fast to the short thread stage (228°F/112°C) on a sugar thermometer; the simple test for this is to dip your thumb and first finger into cold water, then take some of the boiling syrup off a wooden spoon. Draw thumb and finger apart and a short thread of sticky syrup should form between your thumb and finger. It only needs to be ½ in. (1 cm) long. Why one's fingers don't burn, I don't know!

Use the double-bladed knife. Meanwhile, process the mangoes, sieve and set aside. Place egg and yolks in the Magimix and process for about 20 seconds until light and fluffy. With the motor running, pour the boiling hot syrup down the feed tube onto the egg and process for 20–30 seconds. Continue by pouring in the mango purée, the lemon juice and, finally the cream; process for about 20 seconds (no longer or you may turn the cream to butter) and taste to see if there is enough lemon juice.

Turn into a shallow container, preferably metal or tinfoil, and freeze until almost solid. Break up and return to the Magimix and process until absolutely smooth. Turn into a chilled serving dish or container and refreeze. Mellow in the fridge for half an hour or so before serving. Almond Shortbread Fingers (page 17) are good with this.

Mango Ice Cream is easy to make but is also unusual and sophisticated

An Indian Feast or A Curry Lunch

——◄ ✦ ►——

The British involvement with India is more than two centuries old and Indian food has become part of our tradition. Authentic curry, as we rather loosely call it, but really Indian in food in general, has been difficult for most of us to produce because of the seeming complexity of the terms and techniques used, the number of spices needed and the tremendous amount of chopping, slicing and pounding involved. But now, with increased numbers of shops selling the necessary ingredients and the arrival of the Magimix to do so much of the

hard work, real curry has been brought well within everyone's grasp.

Until I went to India as a nomadic student some twenty years ago I thought, like many people, that curry was Sunday's leftover beef in a curry-powder flavoured, flour thickened sauce, probably with some fried onion, diced apple and a few sultanas as a hopeful gesture towards the East. But in India (in spite of only being able to afford to eat from roadside stalls) I discovered what a wealth of different dishes and styles there are. I found that the bubbling

MENU

Meat Dishes

Murghi Moolie (Chicken in Coconut Cream)

Beef Turrcarri (Beef Curry)

Seek Kofta Khasa (Spicy Lamb Meat Balls)

Dum Gosht (Dry Spicy Lamb)

———

Pulse Dishes

Chana Dal (Split Pea Curry)

Chana Dal Finished with Onions and Spices

———

Rice Dishes

Plain Boiled Rice

Spiced Pilau Rice

———

Vegetable Dishes

Baingan Bhurta (Aubergine Purée)

Snack Dishes

Onion Barjias

———

Breads

Pooris

Poppadums

———

Accompanying Dishes and Chutneys

Coconut Chutney

Parsley or Coriander Chutney

Tamarind Chutney

Toasted Coconut

Grated Radish with Black Mustard Seed

Cucumber and Yoghurt

Tomato with Kalonji (onion) seeds

———

Drinks

Lassi

cauldrons of curry and other dishes were far too hot for me; the worst occasion was when I was given a deep-fried chilli as a joke and I thought I was going to die, much to the amusement of my companions. But I discovered *chapatis*, hot from beehive ovens, *Samosas*, stuffed *parathas*, *pakorthas*, *Poori* and *Bhajias* – all snacks, breads or savoury mouthfuls sold from stalls or wandering sellers and drunk with a glass of *lassi*, that cooling yoghurt drink that goes so well with curried dishes. How we survived the germs I shall never know but we did and got an inkling, and it was only an inkling, of what Indian food could really be like and a recent trip to Nepal has helped to increase my love and enjoyment of it.

Gradually I have discovered a bit more, learning to mix my own spices rather than rely on curry powders and learning to balance robust flavours like garlic, onion, turmeric and coriander with the pungents like chilli, ginger and mustard and aromatics such as cardamom, cinnamon, mace and nutmeg. Chilli, by the way, is addictive which I suppose explains peoples' desire for ever hotter dishes. I now appreciate that you feel some spices on the tongue while some tickle up your cheeks; others get you in the back of the throat, there are those that are an aid to digestion and a few that arouse your appetite. My personal bias is towards the aromatics and I now love to prepare fragrant spiced dishes which do not blast the roof off my mouth, bring tears to my eyes or make me break out in beads of unlady-like sweat! Some books on indian cookery do seem to make it all sound incredibly complicated and daunting, going on endlessly about *dumned*, *bhoona*, *talawa*, *korma* or *bhagar* when in fact these words mean braised, sauté, deep-fried, stewed and stir-fried respectively. I propose to use the English phrase that we all understand.

Indian dishes are wonderful for entertaining. Anyone who has been to a curry lunch in the Far East, with old India hands or with the Services will know how many people can be entertained and what a good party it makes; delve into this pot or that, adding the chutneys and accompaniments of your choice from the immense variety laid out on the table. It's a relatively inexpensive way to entertain, and, because many of the dishes can be made before-hand, a particularly useful one for the cook hostess or for after a drinks party.

I have designed this chapter to be used in two ways. First of all, it is a curry feast for twenty or more people; and secondly for newcomers who, until they have cooked all the dishes and know their style, might have difficulty planning a menu. I have made a selection of dishes which I think complement each other and which I hope will be liked. Naturally, all of them can be used on their own, or with just two or three others, to make a good supper for the family or a small party for a few friends. I have searched for dishes that are attractive to the european palate and have cooked them using the correct techniques and ingredients. I can find all the ingredients locally but I have indicated alternatives where there might be difficulties obtaining them and I have mentioned which of them can be stored in the freezer. I have tried all the recipes out on a number of curry addicts who have approved, dubbing them 'gentle in the mouth and warm in the stomach' as all good curries should be. I have also tried to produce dishes which will not only satisfy the knowledgeable but will charm the first time curry cook with their relative simplicity and subtlety of flavour.

Indian cooking is not quicker or easier than our own but as many of the dishes taste even better when reheated, it is often convenient to do much of the work several days beforehand. Many of them freeze well but do remember to use really fresh spices because the freezer will accentuate any mustiness or staleness in a herb or spice. In addition, quite a number of ingredients like coriander, coconut and ginger can be frozen to avoid the need for a last minute visit to a specialist store.

The Beef Turrcarri uses only the simplest ingredients together with curry powder so there is no necessity to get special spices; it's slightly sweet, has been my favourite basic curry for years and is a good one to cut your teeth on; the use of black treacle compensates for the reluctance of most Europeans to fry their onions brown enough to get the right, almost caramelised flavour and colour. Murghi Moolie I love for its mild delicacy and that wonderful flavour of coconut cream with plenty of rich sauce. Dum Gosht is a drier curry with all the herbs, spices and yoghurt clinging to the cubes of lamb and giving them an excellent hot spiciness. Finally, Seek Kofta Khasa, minced lamb, which can be moulded into balls and fried, grilled on skewers or barbecued.

You can have a large party using only one of these four dishes and each would give your meal a complete but different character. But if you want to show off a bit or have a maharajah coming to lunch, do two, three or even all of them and you know you will have a feast of flavours to savour.

Spices, Herbs and Unusual Ingredients Used and How to Store Them

For a very modest sum, you can set yourself up with a range of spices, herbs and ingredients which will open up a whole new world of Indian dishes to you and also be useful in much of your everyday cooking. Those that are bought whole will keep well so it doesn't matter if you don't make these dishes very often but ready ground spices tend to loose their volatile oils quite quickly, leaving them stale and without much flavour. Here is a list of the ones I find most useful, though not an exhaustive list of all the possibilities. All of them are widely available, often being cheapest in an Asian store. I have marked them to be used fresh (§), from the freezer (F) or store cupboard (S); you will see only radish *must* be used fresh and this can easily be substituted by carrot and so lots of visits to specialist stores are not necessary. Some, like chilli, coriander, parsley and ginger are probably nicer if fresh but can very adequately be kept in the freezer. Chop the coriander or parsley in the Magimix and freeze it; grate the still frozen ginger straight from the freezer. If you are using fresh coconut to make Toasted Coconut, Coconut Cream or Milk you will find it much easier with the Magimix than grating or shredding it by hand. If you haven't got time to deal with a fresh coconut or can't get a good one, then a packet of creamed coconut can be kept in your store cupboard as an alternative and

Culpeper do delicious tinned coconut whirls which make an excellent, if more expensive, substitute for toasted coconut.

Warning. When handling, de-seeding or chopping fresh chillies, be very careful not to touch your mouth or eyes with your fingers because the chilli juice on your fingers can burn terribly.

Nicola visiting Fiddes Payne, the Herb and Spice Merchants warehouse

Spices (all S)

Aniseed	Cinnamon (sticks and ground)	Kalonji (onion seed)
Bay Leaf	Cloves (whole and ground)	Mace (blades and ground)
Black Mustard Seeds	Coriander Seeds (whole)	Nutmeg (whole)
Black Peppercorns	Cumin Seeds (whole)	Paprika
Cardamom (pods and ground)	Fennel Seeds	Sesame Seeds
Cayenne Pepper	Garam Masala (a mix of spices)	Turmeric (ground)

Other Ingredients

§ Basil (fresh)	§F Coriander (fresh)	S Mango Chutney
S Basil (dried)	§ Fresh Dill	S Mint (dried)
S Besan Flour (dried pea flour)	S Dried Dill	§F Parsley
S Chana Dal (split peas)	S Garlic	S Poppadums
§F Chillies (fresh)	S Ghee (clarified butter or cooking fat)	S Sesame Oil
S Chillies (dried)		S Tamarind (dried)
§ Coconut (fresh for 1–3 weeks) F or freezer	§F Ginger (fresh root)	§ White Radish or Mooli (fresh)
§F Coconut Cream (fresh)	§ Limes or Lemons (1–3 weeks life)	§ Yoghurt (plain–1 weeks life)
§ Coconut Cream (packet)	S Lime Pickle	

Some Indian Techniques

Frequently, one or more of these methods will be used in one dish to achieve precisely the desired taste.

Roasting Spices. Sometimes spices are heated and tossed in a very heavy, dry frying pan until they darken in colour a little and develop a roasted aroma; they can then be used whole or ground.

Roasting Spices

Popping Spices

Grinding Spices. Many whole spices are ground just before use for maximum freshness. A pestle and mortar suits small quantities or a coffee grinder is ideal to grind larger quantities.

'Popping' Spices. This is really frying whole spices for a moment to release their flavour. They often start popping in the pan, hence the term I use. These larger whole spices, like cinnamon sticks or cloves, are not meant to be eaten but are left, like bay leaves, on the side of the plate.

Pulped Ingredients. Onion, ginger, garlic, chillies or tomatoes are often processed to a pulp, with a little water, before being added to a dish.

———————— : ————————

Some Useful Basic Recipes

Garam Masala. This is a spice mix which you can buy or make for yourself. Your own will tend to be better than the ready made one because you can be more generous with the expensive and aromatic spices. It is not hot like a curry powder, just fragrant and is usually sprinkled over food at the end of its cooking time to give a delicious spicy flavour.

¾ oz (20 g) cardamom seeds in their pods
½ oz (12 g) cinnamon stick
¼ oz (6 g) whole cloves
¼ oz (6 g) cumin seeds
2 blades mace or ¼ teaspoon ground mace
¼ nutmeg, freshly grated

Grind all the spices in a coffee grinder or pound them in a mortar. Sieve very carefully, so you don't get it up your nose, and keep in a tightly stoppered jar, away from light and heat.

Ghee. Clarified butter is used a lot in Indian cooking; with all the milk solids, impurities and salt removed, it will keep almost indefinitely and heat to very high temperatures without burning as well as giving a great taste to dishes. In most instances, vegetable oil can be used instead of ghee but if you are contemplating making a number of Indian dishes, it is worth buying or making some ghee. It is not in the least difficult to make.

½ lb butter, preferably unsalted, but it does not
   really matter.

Chop up the butter and place it in a heavy pan. Heat it very gently until the butter melts, then leave it over a very low heat or on a heat diffuser for up to ½ hour. A froth will come to the top and moisture will evaporate off. You should leave it until the milk solids have dried up and are only golden crumbs on the bottom of the pan but I frequently just skim off the top froth and carefully pour off the golden oil, leaving the milky, salty residue behind (it's delicious in mashed potatoes, but watch, for it can be very salty). The jar of ghee should keep for up to a year and is best used to flavour lentil and rice dishes, or for very fast frying of onions, spices or meat.

Fresh Coconut Cream and Milk

approx. 1 pint (600 ml) cream and milk
1 coconut
13 fl oz (375 ml) boiling water

Choose a heavy feeling coconut with plenty of water inside when you shake it. Drive a skewer into two of the coconut's 'eyes' and shake the water out into a glass. It makes a delicious drink but is neither coconut cream nor milk. Break open the coconut by placing on the ground and hitting sharply round its waist with a hammer or heavy instrument. Check that the coconut is fresh and has not gone off (when it will have a disgusting rancid taste). There was a time when I kept getting so many bad coconuts that I took to cracking them open, much to everyone's amazement, in the shop or on the pavement; there is nothing more annoying than starting to cook a dish, only to find one of your ingredients is 'off'. Once broken into 3–4 pieces, prise the flesh from the shell with an old knife. If you have gas, you can place pieces of coconut, shell side down, directly on the flame for a few minutes to loosen the flesh and make it easier to get out. There is no need to pare off the coconut's brown backing.

Use the double-bladed knife. Place all the bits of coconut in the Magimix bowl and process with the on/off technique until it is very finely chopped indeed. Now pour on 5 fl oz (150 ml) of the boiling water, process again then turn into a cloth or muslin and squeeze out all the liquid vigorously. This is coconut cream and will be quite thick.

Return the coconut to the Magimix, pour over the remaining 8 fl oz (225 ml) of boiling water and process again; you should really leave this for 20–30 minutes but I find the Magimix processes the coconut so finely that you can really squeeze out all the goodness at once. Squeeze out all the liquid again. This is coconut milk. Sometimes the first and second pressing are combined to use in a dish. Both the cream and milk will freeze quite well and so too will the chopped or grated coconut.

Cracking open a coconut

Turning the processed coconut into a muslin cloth

Squeezing out the coconut cream

Murghi Moolie (Chicken in Coconut Cream)

Freshly made coconut cream gives these chicken pieces, in a fragrantly spiced sauce, their delicate flavour; this is one of my favourite dishes and I like to serve it with rice, *poppadums*, tomato slices, toasted coconut and to accompany it courgettes or some other green vegetable. You can substitute packeted coconut cream for the freshly made variety.

for 4–6 people
3½ lb (1.6 kg) chicken
1 pint (600 ml) fresh coconut cream and milk or
    15 fl oz (450 ml) water and 7 oz (200 g) of
    a packet of creamed coconut
2 teaspoons cumin seeds   ⎱
2 teaspoons coriander seeds ⎰ roasted and ground
2 teaspoons ground turmeric

½ lb (225 g) onions
5 cloves garlic
1–2 fresh chillies   ⎫ processed to a
1 in. (2–3 cm) cube peeled   ⎬ paste with the
    fresh root ginger   ⎭ water added
4 tablespoons water
5 tablespoons oil
1 in. (2–3 cm) stick cinnamon
4 whole cloves
3–4 whole cardamom pods
1 teaspoon salt
grated rind and juice of 1–2 limes or 1 lemon

To Finish
1 tablespoon roasted sesame seeds
1 teaspoon roughly crushed black peppercorns

Make the fresh coconut cream and milk as in the basic recipe (page 71).
Use the double-bladed knife. Process the roughly

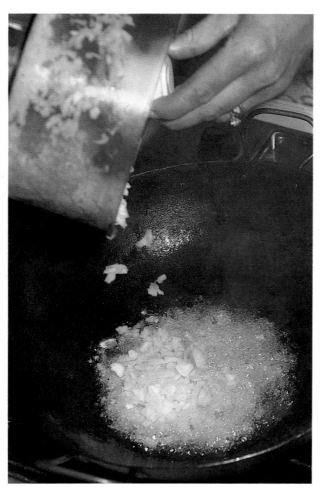

Adding the onion to the 'popped' spices

Stirring the ginger, garlic and chilli mixture into the fried onions

chopped packet of creamed coconut with hot water; mix in the grated lime or lemon rind and juice.

Cut the chicken into 12–16 pieces.

Roast the coriander and cumin seeds in a heavy, dry frying pan until they go a shade or two darker and smell roasted; then grind them, mix with the ground turmeric and set aside.

Slightly flatten the cardamom pods so they just open and set aside with the whole cloves and cinnamon stick.

Use the double-bladed knife. Place the roughly cut up onions in the Magimix bowl and chop finely with the on/off technique. Set aside.

Process the peeled and roughly chopped ginger, skinned garlic and de-seeded chillies (you can leave the seeds in for a hotter dish) in the Magimix, adding 4 tablespoons water to make a pulp. Set aside.

Heat the oil in a heavy casserole or wok and, when hazing, add the cinnamon, whole cloves and slightly flattened cardamom. Let them fry and 'pop' for a moment before adding the finely chopped onion. Fry the onion until it is speckled with brown then stir in the ginger, garlic, chilli pulp, the coriander, cumin and turmeric mix and the salt. Add in the chicken pieces and fry over a moderate heat for 5 minutes or so. Now carefully add in the mixed coconut cream and lime rind and juice, stir well and bring to the simmer; the coconut cream and milk should cover the chicken. Simmer, uncovered, very gently for about 1½ hours until the chicken is tender, or you can cook it in a slow oven (300°F/150°C/Gas 2). Once nearly cooked, it can be left to cool overnight, then re-heated, or it can be frozen.

To Serve. Boil fast for a little to reduce the sauce which should still be fairly copious.

Toast the sesame seeds in a heavy dry frying pan until they jump, colour slightly and give off a roasted smell. Roughly crush the black peppercorns, or grind very coarsely. Scatter the sesame and pepper over the chicken and serve.

The turmeric is added

The chicken pieces are fried in the mixture

Pouring the coconut cream and milk over the chicken

Simmering gently until tender

Beef Turrcarri (Beef Curry)

Turrcarri or curries in India are dishes with plenty of juice or gravy, they are slowly cooked for a long time until the juice is full of flavour and the meat very well cooked. In this recipe I have used no special spices or unusual ingredients so it should be easy enough for anyone to make, and will I hope, lead you on to try further recipes and dishes. It is a slightly sweet curry with a good dark colour, its thickening coming from the onion, apples and tomato purée, not from flour which would be most unauthentic. I put the chillies in whole so you can remove them when the curry is as hot as you like; you can use fresh chillies which will be relatively mild or the dried ones which will be hotter, especially if you leave the seeds in. Beware if you leave the chillies in that someone does not eat them and get their head blasted off! This curry also freezes very well and I often make double quantities, but then I don't quite double up the stock quantity or it will be very runny.

4–6 people
1½ lb (675 g) stewing beef
3 oz (75 g) dripping or lard
12 oz (350 g) onions
2 cooking apples
2–3 tablespoons curry powder (mild Madras or any variety you wish)
2 cloves garlic
1 tablespoon tomato purée
2–4 (or more!) fresh green or dried red chillies (or you could use chilli powder or cayenne pepper)
1 tablespoon black treacle
2 tablespoons sultanas
2 tablespoons chopped lime pickle or chutney
1 bay leaf
¾–1 pint (450–600 ml) beef stock or stock cube and water

Use the standard slicing disc. Halve and slice the onions. Heat the dripping in a large frying pan or casserole, add the onions, fry them to a good brown and remove. Cut the meat into 1 in. (2–3 cm) cubes and roll in the curry powder; add to the pan with the chopped garlic and brown all over without burning the curry powder. Remove and set aside.
Use the double-bladed knife. Peel and core the apples and place them, roughly cut up, in the Magimix bowl. Roughly chop with the on/off technique, add to the casserole and fry for several minutes before returning all the meat, etc. and adding in all the remaining ingredients. If you used a frying pan, turn it all into a casserole at this stage; I use earthenware for slow cooking this sort of dish. Cover and simmer extremely gently for 2–4 hours until the meat is tender, or you can cook it in a slow oven (300°F/150°C/Gas 2). I often remove the lid after a while so the sauce can reduce a little as it cooks. Remove the chillies, though you can leave them in overnight if you are going to re-heat the curry the next day and you want it a little hotter. Most curries, just like stews, seem to taste better when re-heated because the flavours have had time to blend together. Serve with Plain Boiled Rice, Dal if you like, Poppadums or Pooris and side dishes of mango chutney, lime pickle, sliced bananas in lemon juice and any of the chutneys included in this chapter.

——————— : ———————

Seek Kofta Khasa (Spicy Lamb Meat Balls)

These meat balls make a delicious supper served with Pooris or pitta bread (the middle eastern flat bread which is readily available), or Poppadums and Coconut Chutney. They are also good to serve with drinks, on picnics and at barbecue suppers.

for 4–6 people
1 lb (450 g) lean lamb
1 tablespoon grated fresh root ginger
1 clove garlic
1 teaspoon fennel seeds (or use cumin)
4 cardamom pods (seeds removed and pounded) or ¼ teaspoon ground cardamom
¼–½ teaspoon freshly ground black pepper
juice of 1 lime or ½ lemon
2 tablespoons yoghurt
1 teaspoon salt
4–5 tablespoons oil for frying

Pound the fennel and cardamom seeds.
Use the double-bladed knife. Cut the meat into cubes, leave on a little fat but remove any gristle or sinew. Turn on the Magimix and quickly drop the meat

cubes down the tube onto the turning blade; chop finely then add the grated ginger, crushed garlic, pounded fennel and cardamom, pepper, salt and lime or lemon juice. With the motor running add the yoghurt through the feed tube but do not process for too long for, if the mixture is too smooth, the koftas can become dry, once cooked. Using wet hands (a pinch of bicarb in a little water to wet your hands will make the meat stick less) form the mixture into about 24 small balls.

To Fry. Heat the oil in a wide frying pan and fry the koftas, rolling them around until they are a good brown; but fry them quickly, probably in several lots, so that they stay moist and tender in the middle.

To Grill. Mould the mixture around flat kebab skewers in about 3 in. (8 cm) lengths and not more than about 1 in. (2–3 cm) thick. Pre-heat the grill to very hot (or even better, do them over charcoal on the barbecue) and grill them, turning frequently, very close to the heat for about 4–6 minutes. They should be brown on the outside but moist and succulent inside. Serve them with Spiced Pilau Rice and Parsley, Coconut or Tamarind Chutney. They can also be cooked in a spiced onion and yoghurt sauce (as prepared for the Dum Gosht), and are delicious that way too.

Frying the Koftas

Dum Gosht (Dry Spicy Lamb)

Cubes of leg or shoulder of lamb are browned and then slowly braised in a spiced onion and yoghurt sauce. Once tender and cooked, the sauce is reduced away until the lamb is covered in a spicy hot coating. Good served with Spiced Pilau Rice, Chana Dal and Baingan Bhurta.

for 4–6 people

2 lb (900 g) boned leg or shoulder of lamb
6 tablespoons vegetable oil
½ lb (225 g) onions
2 in. (5 cm) cube of peeled fresh root ginger (or ¾ teaspoon ground ginger)
5 cloves garlic
2 oz (50 g) fresh coriander or parsley heads
¼ teaspoon ground cloves
1 tablespoon paprika
5 cardamom pods (the pods removed and the seeds pounded) or ½ teaspoon ground cardamom
1 teaspoon freshly grated nutmeg
1 bay leaf
¼ –½ teaspoon cayenne pepper or ½ teaspoon coarsely ground black peppercorns
8–10 fl oz (225–300 ml) plain yoghurt
4–5 chopped fresh basil leaves or ½ teaspoon dried basil
1 teaspoon salt

To Finish

½ teaspoon *garam masala* or good pinch mace and 1 teaspoon paprika

Cut the meat into 1½ in. (4 cm) cubes, removing quite a lot of the fat if you have used shoulder of lamb. Heat the oil in a wide casserole or frying pan and brown the meat in batches before removing and setting aside.

Use the 4 mm or standard slicing disc. Slice the onions and fry in the oil until a really good brown.

Use the double-bladed knife. Process the ginger and garlic cloves until roughly chopped, then add the fresh coriander or parsley and process until all are finely chopped. Add this to the browned onions and oil and fry for 5–10 minutes; then return the meat and any juices to the pan with the ground cloves, paprika, pounded cardamom, grated nutmeg, cayenne pepper, salt and whole bay leaf and stir and

Frying the cubed lamb

Pouring the basil and yoghurt over the meat

fry for a minute. Stir the basil into the yoghurt and add to the pan off the stove, stirring well as it comes to the simmer. Cover closely and cook in a moderate oven (350°F/180°C/Gas 4) for 1½ hours or until tender. Leave to cool if not serving until the next day. Remove lid and boil fast to evaporate sauce; this may take up to 20 minutes. As it thickens, reduce the heat periodically and stir frequently and carefully to stop it burning. When all the liquid has gone and the mixture is frying again, spoon off some fat, sprinkle with *garam masala* or mace and paprika and serve.

———————— : ————————

Chana Dal (Split Pea Curry)

These large yellow split peas (you can use any variety of lentil or split pea for this dish, just vary the cooking time) have a rich flavour, made softer and rounder by the addition of coconut cream, and I often use the packet coconut for this dish. This recipe is hardly hot at all but you can easily increase the quantity of fresh chilli or add cayenne pepper to your taste. Alternatively, you can finish it with fried brown onions and spices which is also very good. Dal can be quite hot and served accompanied by rice, breads, vegetables and chutneys or it can be blander and used to accompany the hotter curried meat dishes.

for 4–6 people
½ lb (225 g) *chana dal*
¾ pint (450 ml) water

1 small onion
1 or more fresh chillies (de-seeded for milder
    flavour) or pinch–⅛ teaspoon cayenne pepper
1 clove garlic
¼ teaspoon turmeric
2–3 oz (50–75 g) packet coconut cream or
    8 fl oz (225 ml) thick coconut milk
½ teaspoon black peppercorns, roughly crushed
¼ teaspoon cumin seed
½–1 teaspoon salt

Wash and pick over the *dal*, particularly removing any tiny stones that may be amongst it, then soak overnight in plenty of cold water; alternatively, cover with water and bring to the boil; boil for 1 minute, remove from heat and leave to stand for 1 hour before draining and continuing. Place in a heavy casserole or saucepan and cover with the water. Bring gently to the boil then skim off the heavy scum that these *dal* throw and leave simmering while you prepare the onion, etc.
Use the double-bladed knife. Add the roughly chopped onion, garlic and fresh chilli to the Magimix and chop finely with the on/off technique. Add to the pan of skimmed *chana dal* together with the turmeric and simmer, covered but with the lid just ajar, for about 1½ hours or until the *dal* is absolutely tender but not breaking up. Stir fairly frequently towards the end so the *dal* does not stick to the pan as the water reduces. Once tender, stir in the coconut cream in little pieces or add the fresh coconut milk and simmer until of a nice thick porridge consistency (though the grains of *dal* should remain whole); then add the crushed peppercorns, cumin and salt to taste. Pulses are always salted towards the end of their cooking time so that they do not toughen and take much longer to cook.

Chana Dal Finished with Onions and Spices

Follow the last recipe to soak and cook the *chana dal* with just the water, onion, garlic, chilli or cayenne and turmeric until tender.

To Finish
2–3 tablespoons *ghee* or vegetable oil
2 onions
1 clove garlic
1 tablespoon grated ginger
½ tea21 1½ teaspoons *garam masala*
⅛–¼ teaspoon cayenne pepper
½–1 teaspoon salt

Use the standard slicing disc. Slice the onions. Heat the *ghee* or oil in a frying pan and fry the onions until they are really well browned. Add the garlic and ginger and continue to fry until they too brown

lightly. Draw all this to the side of the pan, or remove and heat the *ghee* or oil until very hot; throw in the cumin seeds (they should pop and jump almost at once), draw the pan off the stove and add *garam masala* and cayenne. Stir all together for a moment, then pour this mixture into the *dal*, stir round and serve.

———————— : ————————

Plain Boiled Rice

There are many ways of cooking rice. The one I choose for serving with curry is to cook the rice in plenty of boiling salted water so the surface starch on each grain of rice is washed off. The water becomes thick and cloudy but the rice, when drained, is light and fluffy.

for 4–6 people
8–12 oz (225–350 g) long grain rice
3½ pints (2.1 l) water
2 teaspoons salt

Bring the water to the boil in a large saucepan and salt it; then add the rice, stir once and boil fast for approximately 10–15 minutes without it boiling over; remove a grain of rice and try it; it should be firm between your teeth but cooked right through.

Drain the rice into a colander, rinse with hot water and let it drain again before turning into a serving dish. Cover and keep warm until ready to serve. When cooking for a large party, I often cook the rice the day before. Cook it as above but rinse it with cold water and leave to drain for 5 minutes before turning into a shallowish dish and covering with tinfoil. This rice will re-heat perfectly in a moderately hot oven (375°F/190°C/Gas 5) in 30 minutes, turning sides to the middle with a fork once or twice.

For a large party of about 20 people, I would allow 2–2½ lb (900 g–1.15 kg) or 1½ lbs (675 g) if I were doing a double size pilau as well. Cook it in masses of water, or in several batches if you have no really large pans and, if you are going to re-heat it, allow about 1 hour for this.

Full of Eastern Promise!

Spiced Pilau Rice

In a pilau the rice is fried to seal on a layer of surface starch so the finished dish is not sticky. It is then cooked, with just the correct amount of measured stock or water, so the rice ends up perfectly tender, moist but not wet and with every grain separate. Many flavours and ingredients can be introduced into a pilau and chicken, vegetable or meat are often cooked with it. *Basmati* rice makes a delicous pilau though you can use any rice. I tend to choose a golden coloured rice, which seems to me to cook better than a very white one, and I frequently buy pre-prepared 'easy-cook' rice which saves a lot of washing, soaking, draining and drying. This pilau is spiced with the classic combination of cardamom, cloves and cinnamon which are 'popped' in hot oil or *ghee* before the rice is added (these whole spices are not meant to be eaten but are picked out, like the cloves in apple pie, and left on the side of the plate).

for 4–6 people
8 oz (225 g) *Basmati* or long grain 'easy-cook' rice
2 tablespoons *ghee* or vegetable oil
4 whole cardamom
8 whole cloves
1 in. (2–3 cm) stick cinnamon
good pinch freshly grated nutmeg
1 finely chopped onion
¾ pint (450 ml) chicken stock or water and stock
    cube
½–1 teaspoon salt (depending on saltiness of stock)

Heat the *ghee* or oil in a casserole until very hot and hazing, then throw in the cardamoms (flattened and opened a little), cloves and cinnamon. Let them 'pop' and fry for a moment before adding the chopped onion. Fry until golden then add the rice and fry for 2–3 minutes until every grain of rice glistens and goes slightly opaque. Now add the stock gradually, so the whole lot does not boil furiously, and then the nutmeg and salt; stir once, cover tightly and cook in a moderate oven (350°F/180°C/Gas 4) for 18–20 minutes. You can also (if you have a nice heavy pan) simmer it very, very gently on top of the stove for 20–30 minutes or sometimes I put it in a very slow oven (225°F/110°C/Gas ½) for about 1½ hours. To test when cooked, remove the lid and take a few grains of rice from the centre; they should be perfectly cooked and no liquid should remain but boil fast for a moment or two if it is too moist. I find

this pilau will keep warm in a very slow oven or on a hot plate for an hour or so without spoiling.
To serve. Loosen and stir the rice with a fork to mix in the spices and serve with *Kebabs*, *Koftas*, *Dum Gosht* or *Chana Dal*.

———————— : ————————

Baingan Bhurta (Aubergine Purée)

Aubergine is baked in the oven until soft then made into a purée and flavoured with coriander, paprika and aniseed. It makes a delicious accompaniment for any of the curries or can just be served with *Chana Dal*, *Pooris* and yoghurt.

for 4–6 people
1½ lb (675 g) medium sized aubergines
4 tablespoons vegetable oil
1 small onion
2 tablespoons coriander seeds
1 teaspoon paprika
1 teaspoon aniseed or fennel or cumin
small handful parsley heads
juice of half lemon
1 teaspoon salt

Prick the aubergines with a fork in 2–3 places and bake in a hot oven (425°F/220°C/Gas 7) for 20–30 minutes until completely tender. Meanwhile, roast the coriander seeds in a heavy dry frying pan for several minutes until they darken and smell roasted; pound together with the aniseed in a mortar or grind them in a coffee grinder. If it looks husky, I usually sieve this quantity of coriander to remove the outer coating which never quite grinds down in a mortar and can be a bit chewy.
Use the double-bladed knife. Chop the onion with the on/off technique and soften it in the oil without browning.

Cut the aubergines in half and scrape all the flesh off the skin into the Magimix; add in the softened onion and its oil, the parsley heads, coriander, paprika, aniseed and salt and process to a smooth purée; drip in the lemon juice and check the seasoning. Serve hot or cold.

Onion Bhajias

These sliced onions in a spiced batter, deep fried by the spoonful, make a delicious snack or side dish, but they do really need last minute deep frying.

for 4–6 people
8 oz (225 g) onions
deep fat for frying

Batter
6 oz (175 g) *besan* (split pea flour) or plain flour or
    half and half plain and wholemeal flour
½ teaspoon ground turmeric
1 fresh chilli (de-seeded for a milder flavour) or
    ⅛ – ¼ teaspoon cayenne pepper
1 teaspoon cumin seed
1 teaspoon *garam masala*
4–5 fl oz (100–150 ml) water
1 teaspoon salt

Use the 4 mm slicing disc. Halve or quarter the onions, slice and set aside.

Batter. *Change to the double-bladed knife.* Place the flour, turmeric, de-seeded and finely chopped chilli or cayenne, cumin seed, *garam masala* and salt in the Magimix bowl and process; then add water to make a fairly stiff batter, like double cream.

Combine onions and batter. The onions should be just nicely coated, not too sticky (add a drop or two of water if they are) and not too runny. Heat the deep fat and, when very hot and hazing (390°F/195°C on a sugar thermometer), deep fry spoonfuls of onions in batter a few at a time, to make crisp brown *bhajias*. Drain on kitchen paper and serve piping hot though they are also good cold and can be taken on picnics.

The fat must be very hot for frying the Bhajias

Poori (Puffed Indian Bread)

This Indian bread dough is so easily made in the Magimix, the kneading being done in less than one minute. After resting and rolling, the pooris can be deep fried when they will puff up in the most amazing way. They can also be cooked in a heavy dry frying pan or on a griddle and will bubble but not puff. Children adore them as a snack and have been known to eat them covered in syrup! They can be rolled and frozen, individually packed, then can be fried straight from the freezer.

I rather like to use a tablespoon of sesame oil in the mixture because, although not authentic, it does give them a lovely flavour. I suspect olive oil or walnut oil would also be rather good.

12 Pooris
4 oz (100 g) plain flour
4 oz (100 g) wholemeal flour
1 tablespoon vegetable oil } or use all
1 tablespoon sesame oil } vegetable oil
3–4 fl oz (75–100 ml) water
½ teaspoon salt

Use the double-bladed knife. Place the flours and salt in the Magimix bowl and process for a moment; then trickle the oils over the flour and process again to incorporate. With the machine running, gradually pour in the water to make a very firm dough; it is best if the mixture stays in polystyrene like granules. Continue processing for about 45 seconds to knead and, if it's still in granules, press together into a dough; or if too dry, you might need to drip in a little additional water, but keep the dough firm. Knead by hand until smooth, form into a ball and rest in a plastic bag for 30 minutes. Divide the dough into twelve equal pieces and keep in a plastic bag. Take each piece and form into a ball, then roll to a 5–5½ in. (12–14 cm) circle. Use as little flour as possible for rolling if you are deep frying the *pooris* or the flour will fall off and cloud your oil. Pile the *pooris* up with cling film between each and keep covered.

Heat the oil until very hot and just smoking; carefully lower a *poori* into the oil; it will sink but as it rises again, duck it back under with a slotted spoon, pressing it down at the edges; also spoon and splash oil over the top to help it puff. Once well puffed, turn over and cook for about 10 seconds on the second

Rolling the balls of Poori dough into neat circles

side. It should be firm by now so lift from the oil and drain over the oil for a moment before laying on kitchen paper to drain further. *Pooris* are best served straight from the pan though they can all be made, layered with kitchen paper to absorb the oil and kept warm.

—————— : ——————

Poppadums

Poppadums are extremely difficult to make and are always bought ready made. Luckily they are easy to cook; fried for a moment in very hot oil, they will almost double in size and become very light and crisp. You can buy them plain or spiced, flavoured with cumin, garlic or pepper. I like to cook them well ahead to have time to get rid of the smell of frying; they will keep (even overnight) if they are left in a warm place where the atmosphere won't make them soften. If you put two in a pan together, they will stay flat as they expand and will be not only quicker to cook but easier to stack afterwards.

packet of *poppadums*
oil for deep frying

Heat the oil until just smoking (390°F/195°C) then take two *poppadums* (scissor tongs are good for this) and place in the oil; push them down so every bit of the *poppadum* goes into the oil and they will immediately grow and spread; remove them after a moment and before they brown. Hold draining above the oil for a second then lay on kitchen paper to drain; blot on the upper side if oil accumulates. Stack them up in a great pile on a plate. Cook them in quick succession so the oil does not overheat. If the oil is not hot enough, they will either not expand properly or, if they do, will be greasy. If you only want to cook a few and don't want to use the deep fryer, they can be cooked in about ¾ in. (1–2 cm) of hot oil in a frying pan. You will have to tip the pan and turn them round and round to get all the edges into the oil, and only do one at a time.

—————— : ——————

Coconut Chutney

A mild cooling dish that can either be served as it is or mixed with yoghurt for a creamy chutney.

1 bowlful
4 oz (100 g) fresh coconut
1 oz (25 g) sesame seeds
grated rind and juice of 1 orange
grated rind and juice of 1 lime or ½ lemon
1 bay leaf
good shake or pinch cayenne pepper
6–8 tablespoons plain yoghurt (optional, to make a
   creamy chutney)

Use the double-bladed knife. Break a really dry bay leaf up finely and place in the Magimix bowl with the broken up coconut and sesame seeds. Process until very finely chopped, then add the grated rinds and juice of the orange and lime or lemon and a little cayenne. Process briefly again, then turn the mixture into a saucepan and heat, stirring, for a few minutes. Cool the coconut mixture and either serve it as it is or fold in the yoghurt to make a creamy mixture. Delicious served with *Pooris* and *Seek Kofta Khasa* or with any of the curried dishes.

Parsley or Coriander Chutney

A fresh cooling chutney, nice made with either parsley or coriander but a chutney which needs to be eaten freshly made.

1 bowlful
a good big handful of parsley or fresh coriander
    leaves
1 teaspoon grated fresh root ginger
1–1½ tablespoons lime or lemon juice
shake or pinch cayenne pepper to your taste
5–6 tablespoons plain yoghurt
½ teaspoon salt

Use the double-bladed knife. Chop the parsley or coriander finely then add the grated ginger, lime or lemon juice, cayenne, salt and yoghurt; process again until well mixed but not completely smooth. Turn into a bowl and serve with *Dum Gosht*, *Beef Turcarri* or *Seek Kofta Khasa*.

———————— : ————————

Tamarind Chutney

Tamarind is long pod with a very sour fibrous pulp in which are embedded numerous mahogany coloured, thumb nail sized seeds; these are a very comforting shape to suck when found in the centre of sweet tamarind balls – a Caribbean confection that I yearn for. Tamarind is said to have the highest acid and sugar content of any fruit and is used to acidulate dishes and to make a sour chutney.

Once you have tasted the sour sweet flavour of tamarind, I think you will want it again. It makes an unusual sour chutney, is one that would be very time consuming to prepare without a Magimix and which adds a very good note to all these dishes.

Tamarind chutney should be used freshly made though it will keep for up to two days. The tamarind is bought in blocks which should be slightly squishy.

1 bowlful
4 oz (100 g) dried tamarind
10 fl oz (300 ml) water

1 tablespoon grated fresh root ginger or ½ teaspoon
    ground ginger
1 clove garlic
1 tablespoon sugar
½ teaspoon *garam masala*
good shake or pinch cayenne pepper
¼ teaspoon salt

Use the plastic mixing blade. Break up and soak the dried tamarind, seeds and all, in the water for ½ hour. Drain off, but keep, the water. Turn the pulp, still complete with seeds, into the Magimix bowl and process (never mind the rattling of the seeds), gradually adding in the water until you have a smooth pulp. Push this pulp through a sieve to separate seeds and fibre. Stir in the grated ginger, garlic (put through a garlic press), sugar, *garam masala*, cayenne and salt, and turn into a bowl to serve.

———————— : ————————

Grated Radish or Mooli with Black Mustard Seed

The huge crunchy sweet white mooli or radish, now often available at the greengrocer or in the specialist Asian shops, makes a very good salad when grated. Here we dress it with black mustard seeds or cumin seeds which have been 'popped' in hot oil to make a crunchy fresh accompaniment for Indian dishes.

1 bowl
½–¾ lb (225–350 g) fresh white mooli or radish
    (you could use carrot)
2 tablespoons vegetable oil
1 tablesoon black mustard seed or 2 teapoons cumin
good squeeze lime or lemon juice
salt

Use the coarse grating disc. Peel the radish and cut into segments to fit sideways down the tube. Grate and turn into a bowl, sprinkle with salt and lemon juice. Heat the oil in a small frying pan until just smoking, then add the mustard seed which will begin to 'pop' in a moment. Pour them and the oil over the radish and toss. Serve warm or cold.

Toasted Coconut

I first started making this when staying with a friend in Barbados but it was a long slow job, shaving the coconut into thin strips with a potato peeler! With the Magimix, it's a moment's task and makes absolutely delicious nibbles for drinks parties as well as accompanying curried dishes to perfection.

1 bowl
1 coconut
salt

Remove the coconut from the shell in large pieces as in the basic recipe for Fresh Coconut Cream (page 71).

Use the standard slicing disc. Pack the feed tube with upright standing pieces of coconut and slice, using the most delicate pressure on the pusher to make the thinnest possible shavings of coconut. Spread these fine coconut slices on a baking sheet and bake in a moderate oven (350°F/180°C/Gas 4) until they are golden and crisp. You will have to toss and turn them from time to time and they will take from ½–1 hour, depending on the quantity and juiciness of the coconut. Salt the toasted coconut and keep in an airtight tin.

Cucumber and Yoghurt

Cucumber and yoghurt make such a cooling combination, and not only on the tongue. The fresh green and cream look lifts the eye when seen against the heavy brown of so many curried dishes.

1 large bowl
1 cucumber
1 fresh chilli (de-seeded for milder flavour) or pinch
    cayenne pepper
1 clove garlic
¼–½ pint (150–300 ml) plain yoghurt
1 tablespoon fresh chopped dill or coriander leaves
good squeeze lime or lemon juice
1 teaspoon salt

Use the 4 mm slicing disc. Cut the cucumber in half then cut each half into four, lengthways. Pack these strips into the feed tube and slice with moderate pressure so you get flat dice of cucumber. Lay in a colander, sprinkle with salt and leave for ½ hour with a plate and weights on top.

Stir the finely chopped chilli or cayenne into the yoghurt then add a clove of garlic, put through a garlic press, and the chopped dill or coriander leaves (use dried dill if no fresh is available). Drain the

The coconut 'shaved' with the standard slicing disc . . .

. . . and toasted to a delicate brown

The cucumber cut into large triangular sections

The 4mm slicing disc is used to cut the cucumber

cucumber well and add with a good squeeze of lime or lemon juice. Correct seasoning and turn into a bowl. Decorate with dill or coriander leaves.

———— : ————

Tomatoes with Kalonji (Onion) Seeds

A touch of tomato colour looks good amongst the chutneys. I like to serve them just sliced and sprinkled with *kalonji* seeds because the black specks on the tomato look and taste rather nice. But you could also serve them scattered with chopped fresh or dried basil, which although not often used in India, grows abundantly there as a perennial.

1 bowlful
½ lb (225 g) tomatoes
¼–½ teaspoon *kalonji* seeds

Skin the tomatoes and slice thinly. Arrange in a flattish dish and scatter over the *kalonji* seeds.

Lassi

A refreshing yoghurt drink which is wonderful with hot curries or as a refreshing pick-me-up when bought from the wandering sellers in the hot markets and streets of India. It can be sweet or savoury. I prefer the savoury one with salt, mint and a sprinkle of ground cardamom on top.

1 glass
¼ pint (150 ml) plain yoghurt
¼ pint (150 ml) iced water
pinch dried mint
salt to taste

To Garnish
sprig of mint
pinch of ground cardamom

Use the double-bladed knife. Process the yoghurt, water, mint and salt together and turn into a glass. Decorate with a sprig of mint and serve, well iced, with a tiny sprinkle of cardamom on top.

A Childrens' Tea Party

MENU

Hot Fish Bullets
Hot Sausages (no recipe)

———

Egg Mayonnaise Sandwiches
Sardine Sandwiches
Cream Cheese and Chutney Sandwiches

———

Name Place Biscuits
Little Iced Cup Cakes
Button Biscuits
Merry-Go-Round Birthday Cake
Cherry Moments

———

Fresh Fruit Jellies
Vanilla Ice Cream (page 31)
Banana Milk Shake
Orange Apple Fizz (page 105)

Other Things to Remember
Straws
Candles and candle-holders (non-blow
    candles are rather an amusing gimmick)
Paper Napkins
Balloons
Crackers
Paper Hats
Streamers
Tea or Reviving Drinks for Mothers

I'm so thankful I have still got one little one. The others now demand more sophisticated or unusual parties so I'm glad that, at least once a year, we can have a real childrens' party. I try to make the table look as pretty and gay as I can with the food looking attractive and bright; little mouthfuls for little people and everything chosen to amuse and entertain, with tastes to titillate young appetites. I have watched carefully and always notice that children are very conservative in their tastes, are mad on sweets but like some tasty savoury things as well. The days are past when all good children ate bread and butter and sandwiches before being allowed a dig at the tantalising delights on other plates. A pity really, for it was whilst munching your way through the interminable bread and butter that you built up such a tremendous desire for one of those pink iced cakes in the middle of the table and when you got it, how you enjoyed it. Now it is reach for it, nibble it and, as like as not, leave it. To counteract this, and to end up with not too much debris on the plates, I make everything as small as possible; if they leave something, it is not a great waste, and if they like something, they can say proudly, 'Do you know, I ate ten of those cherry biscuits!'

I like to have food on the table as well as on plates; little piles of raisins just within reach are like something out of Hansel and Gretel; eating your way along a trail of salted peanuts is rather fun (though some people say really small children shouldn't have these) and so is bejewelling your fingers with those tiny ring biscuits and eating them off one by one. It makes it rather easier for you if they can plough on with plenty within their reach because you may find yourself coping single-handed with the drinks, the child that's feeling a little lost, the two toughies who are terrorising one end of the table and finally, of course, cutting the birthday cake.

Cutting the cake!

As always, planning and cooking ahead will be a great help for there are always so many things to do like blowing up the balloons, cooking the sausages and finally dressing your own children at the last minute so you don't have a Tom Kitten episode on your hands. If your party is for hefty ten year old boys, you don't want everything too small or it will look as though a plague of locusts has descended within the first five minutes. But for the smaller ones, search for the tiny petit four paper cases, rather than the regular size, so you can do really small Little Iced Cup Cakes. Tiny sausages are a must and I find as every child is brought up on and loves fish fingers (not really suitable for tea party), they enjoy the little deep-fried Fish Bullets which they can eat off toothpicks or in their fingers. Small sandwiches are also a must and I rely on the classics that I used to enjoy most as a child – sardine, egg, and cream cheese and chutney. What could be better? You could even freeze the sardine ones as well as the Fish Bullets, sausages and birthday cake base and don't forget to cover the piled plates, ready on the table, with cling-film to keep them fresh and moist, only whipping it off as the first child gets to the table.

Jellies are essential (it's not a childrens' party without them) so I have given a recipe for a Fresh Fruit Jelly, and ice cream is usually popular. You'll probably have bought this in a big tub but if you wanted home made, the Vanilla Ice Cream is not too rich. I like to go a bit mad with the icing, mixing up a rainbow of three or four colours and using them to decorate as many things as possible. Name Place Biscuits, which each child finds on its plate, can be highly decorative and are firm enough to be taken home without breaking. The Little Iced Cup Cakes, Button Biscuits and the Merry-Go-Round Birthday Cake can all be iced in the same matching colours which helps to give the party a theme and the table a more cohesive look, especially if you can find balloons that match.

Crackers, paper hats and streamers ensure that the children are in a suitably relaxed mood for the rigours of musical bumps, pass the parcel, the magician or whatever follows and don't forget to have at least a cup of tea on hand when the parents come to collect.

Hot Fish Bullets

These little balls of smoked fish and potato, deep fried to a crispy brown, appeal to children who also love the name. Fry them ahead, then reheat for parties and serve on tooth picks. For grown up parties, you can add a little curry powder, spices or onion. Kept in the freezer, they are very useful for teas or suppers and make a change from the endless fish fingers. It is essential to make them with old floury potatoes and not to process for too long in the Magimix, for mashed potato can go completely sticky and gluey if over-processed.

20–25 bullets
8 oz (225 g) smoked haddock
10–12 oz (275–350 g) peeled potatoes
2–3 sprigs parsley
1 egg yolk
salt and pepper
flour
1 egg
breadcrumbs
oil for frying

Place the fish in a saucepan and just cover with cold water. Bring to the boil then draw off the stove and leave for 5–10 minutes until cooked. Boil the potatoes in salted water.

Use the double-bladed knife. Chop the parsley first then roughly break up the fish and potatoes into the Magimix. Add seasoning (but not too much salt for the fish can be quite salty) and the egg yolk. Process with the on/off technique fairly briefly until the fish is broken up, the potato mashed and the whole has drawn together into a smooth mixture. Turn onto a greased plate, cover and leave until cold.

Place flour on one plate, the egg whisked with a few drops of oil and some salt in a shallow bowl (the oil makes the crust crisp and the salt breaks down the egg for even coating) and breadcrumbs on another plate.

Form teaspoonfuls of the fish mixture into large marble sized balls then roll first in flour, then in egg and finally in breadcrumbs. Lay out on kitchen paper until ready to fry (or freeze).

Heat either a deep fat fryer or about 1 in. (2–3 cm) of oil in a deep frying pan. Heat until very hot, about (360°F/180°C), and cook the fish balls, not too many at a time, until a crisp golden brown. (You can also form the mixture into larger conventional fish cakes and shallow fry them). They are very tasty cold for cocktails or a picnic or can be re-heated for 5–10 minutes in a hot oven.

They can also be fried straight from the freezer and make a nice lunch dish served with tomato sauce. Tomato ketchup, tartare sauce or Chinese Hoi Sin sauce are also good with them as a dipping sauce.

Coating the Fish Bullets for frying

Pierce each Fish Bullet with a stick for easy eating

Sandwiches

All good little children start tea with a sandwich and what is better than a well filled, fresh sandwich? Children generally find the vividly coloured cakes more appealing but then return to these tasty sandwiches to fill up. I sometimes also include crushed banana and honey sandwiches for those who like something sweet.

Egg Filling
for 4 rounds (8 slices)
2 hard boiled eggs
1–2 tablespoons mayonnaise
salt and pepper

Use the double-bladed knife. Process the roughly cut up eggs with the mayonnaise and seasoning until finely chopped. Butter the bread, fill the sandwiches, remove crusts (or not as you wish) and cut each round into four squares or triangles or into fingers.

Sardine Filling
for 5–6 rounds (10–12 slices)
1 tin sardines
3 oz (75 g) soft butter
squeeze lemon juice
salt and pepper

Use the double-bladed knife. Process the butter until smooth then add in the drained sardines, seasoning and a squeeze of lemon juice. Process until well creamed. You do not need butter for these sandwiches but fill the bread generously.

Cream Cheese and Chutney Filling
for 5 rounds (10 slices)
4 oz (100 g) cream cheese
1 tablespoon tomato ketchup
1–2 tablespoons tomato chutney
salt and pepper

Use the double-bladed knife. Process all together to combine and chop the chutney. Taste, adjust seasoning and make up the sandwiches.

Name Place Biscuits

A personal biscuit with your name piped on in pretty icing is rather fun to find on your place at the party table. It can be taken home and will keep for ages if it does not get nibbled! The same mixture, with the addition of some ginger, can be used to make a gingerbread house for Christmas.

Spicy Biscuit Mix
approx 21 biscuits 3 × 2½ in. (8 × 6 cm)
6 oz (175 g) honey
1½ oz (35 g) lard
1 oz (25 g) sugar
8 oz (225 g) plain flour
2 oz (50 g) cornflour
½ teaspoon ground cinnamon
pinch ground cloves
pinch ground cardamom (optional)
grated rind 1 lemon
½ teaspoon baking powder
½ whisked egg
few drops lemon essence (optional)
pinch salt

Use the double-bladed knife. Warm the honey, lard and sugar in a saucepan until the sugar has melted. Place all the dry ingredients in the Magimix bowl and process to sift and mix; add the cooled honey mixture and egg and process to a smooth pliable dough in about 20–30 seconds. Form into a flat disc and chill in the polythene bag in fridge for 1–2 hours.

Roll into a rectangle about 9 × 18 in. (22 × 45 cm) on a floured board and cut into 3 × 2½ in. (8 × 6 cm) rectangles. Lay on a greased baking sheet and cook in a moderate oven (350°F/180°C/Gas 4) for 10–15 minutes until pale golden and cooked; cool on a rack.

Ice using Four differrent Coloured Icings.

First dilute some of the white icing and coat the biscuits with a thin layer, using a pastry brush. Let them dry before decorating around the borders in various colours. Then write the childrens' names across the centres, using a fine writing nozzle. Dry completely before storing in a tin.

Four Coloured Icings for Name Place Biscuits, Little Cup Cakes and Button Biscuits

To keep the same gay colour theme, I like to ice the cakes and biscuits in pink, blue, green and white which gives a very pretty effect. The colours suit equally well for boys or girls. It is easiest if you have 4 small piping bags and changeable nozzles.

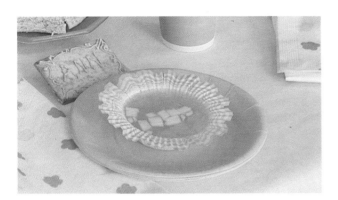

2 egg whites
12 oz (350 g) sifted icing sugar
good squeeze lemon juice
few drops red colouring
few drops blue colouring
few drops green colouring

You will need
1 or preferably 4 small piping bags
1 fine (writing) nozzle
1 medium rose nozzle

Use the double-bladed knife. Place the egg whites in the Magimix bowl with a squeeze of lemon juice. Process for 5 seconds then add the sifted icing sugar. Process to a stiff white icing, adding more sifted icing sugar if it's not stiff enough to pipe. Divide the mixture between four bowls. Leave one white; colour one pink with a few drops of red colour, adding the colour very carefully from the point of a skewer, a drop at a time so you don't overdo it. Colour one lot blue and the last lot green. Keep each bowl inside a polythene bag when not using so it does not dry out. It will keep for several days.

Little Cup Cakes. Spread the top of each cake with a little icing, thinned if necessary with a drop of water.

Button Biscuits. Pipe a generous rose of icing onto each biscuit, doing some biscuits in each colour.

Icing the Name Place Biscuits

A pretty way of showing each child where to sit

Little Iced Cup Cakes

Button Biscuits

Little Iced Cup Cakes

I like to make these in paper petit four cases so they are really tiny, and to ice them in different colours so they are very bright and attractive.

about 24 cakes
1 egg
the weight of the egg in soft butter, castor sugar and
    self raising flour
pinch of baking powder
little pinch salt
¼ teaspoon vanilla essence
1–1½ tablespoons milk

Use the double-bladed knife. Place all the ingredients in the bowl. Process for 6–8 seconds. Scrape the mixture down from the sides and process for a further 2–4 seconds only or until completely mixed.

Half fill the paper cases with a teaspoonful of the mixture and cook in a moderate oven (350°F/180°C/Gas 4) for about 10 minutes until risen, golden and springy. Cool on a rack and ice with different coloured icings.

Button Biscuits

This short biscuit dough can be rolled and cut into all shapes and sizes and as there is no liquid in it it keeps its shape very well when cut. I cut these into little buttons about 1¼ in. (3 cm) in diameter and, when cooked, pipe them with rosettes of different coloured icings.

approx 50–60 biscuits of 1¼ in. (3 cm) diameter
2½ oz (65 g) soft butter
1¼ oz (30 g) castor sugar
3½ oz (85 g) plain flour
1 egg yolk
½ teaspoon vanilla essence or some grated lemon
    rind

Use the double-bladed knife. Place all the ingredients in the bowl and process for 6–8 seconds. Stop and scrape the bowl down and process for a further 2–4 seconds.

Form the dough into a flat disc. Chill, wrapped, in the fridge for 10 minutes for easy rolling then roll out thinly on a floured board. At this stage I put the whole board in the freezer for a few moments until the dough stiffens because it is then so much easier to handle the little biscuits.

Cut with a circle or shaped cutter into rounds or all sorts of shapes and place on a baking sheet. Bake in a moderate oven (350°F/180°C/Gas 4) for about 7–10 minutes until evenly golden brown, cool on a rack and ice when cold.

————— : —————

Merry-Go-Round Birthday Cake

This all-time favourite, orange victoria sponge cake can be made to look so pretty for a party with its merry-go-round top, its candy sticks, its ribbons and its animal ornaments. Make this cake by the

The all-in-one cake mixture makes the little cup cakes quick and easy to prepare

Magimix all-in-one method, beating all the ingredients together, but you must have the butter as soft as it can be without melting, so soft it plops off the spoon with a tiny shake.

two 10 in. (25 cm) cakes
4 eggs
the weight of the eggs in soft butter and castor sugar
the weight of the eggs minus ½ oz (12 g) in self raising flour
½ teaspoon baking powder
a pinch salt
1 teaspoon grated orange rind
4 tablespoons orange juice

Orange Butter Cream
4 oz (100 g) soft butter
10 oz (125 g) sifted icing sugar
grated rind 1 orange
2 tablespoons marmalade or orange juice

Heat the oven to moderately hot (375°F/190°C/ Gas 5). Sift the flour and baking powder together and grease and flour two 10 in. (25 cm) sandwich tins.
Use the double-bladed knife. Place the very soft butter, castor sugar, eggs, sifted flour and baking powder, salt, orange rind and orange juice in the bowl. Process for 6–8 seconds. Scrape the mixture down from the sides and process for a further 2–4 seconds only or until completely mixed.

Divide the mixture between the two prepared tins, spread it evenly and bake for 20–25 minutes in the pre-heated oven. Remove when golden brown and the cake springs back when touched and is shrinking from the sides of the tin. Leave in the tins for a few minutes before turning out to cool on a wire rack. When cold, sandwich together with half the orange butter cream and spread the top with the remaining cream.
Orange Butter Cream. *Use the double-bladed knife.* Process the butter until creamy and soft, add the sifted icing sugar, orange rind and marmalade or juice and process to a nice creamy consistency (add a few drops of hot water if necessary).

To Decorate the Cake
1 cake frill
12 in. (30 cm) circular cake board
one 11 in. (27 cm) diameter circle of card
pretty paper to cover it
glue
1 in. (2 cm) piece of blu-tack or plasticine
6–8 ornaments or figures
1 stick striped rock ½ in. (1 cm) diameter × 6 in. (15 cm)
6–8 striped drinking straws or thin striped candy sticks
4–5 × 20 in. (50 cm) lengths coloured ¼ in. (½ cm) wide ribbons
1 toothpick
candles and holders

I use 3–4 co-ordinating colours of tissue paper, cut into numerous 2½ in. (6 cm) diameter circles. These are folded into four and stuck on to the roof, over-lapping like tiles; it is fiddly but gives a good effect. You could otherwise stick 8 segments of coloured paper onto the card or cover it with any suitable pretty paper.

First cut to the centre of the card circle, over-lapping the edges by 1 in. (2–3 cm) and glue or staple together. This gives you a slightly conical roof. Starting at the rim, stick on quartered circles of tissue paper, mixing the colours at random, letting the first row overlap the edge of the card a little; continue round and round, overlapping each row until the card is completely covered.

Pin a bought or made cake frill around the cake.

Set the stick of rock firmly into the centre of the cake and round the edge set the striped drinking

Toy rocking horses give the final touch to the cake

straws or thin striped candy sticks, alternating them with the candles and holders. Small decorations go onto the cake, larger ones around it on the cake board. Make a little flag with coloured paper glued to the toothpick then spike the centre of the ribbons onto the toothpick. Put the blob of blu-tack or plasticine inside the conical roof and set it carefully on the central stick of rock; adjust the lengths of the candy sticks or straws around the edge by pushing them deeper into the cake and carefully set the toothpick flag, with its ribbons in place, in the centre of the roof. Arrange the ribbons around the cake. Remove the roof when it is time to light the candles.

—————— : ——————

Cherry Moments

Crisp cookies, rolled in crumbled Weetabix and with a cherry in the middle, are fun for the children to help make and they keep well in tin or freezer.

15–20 cookies
2½ oz (65 g) lard
1½ oz (35 g) soft butter or margarine
3 oz (75 g) castor sugar
½ whisked egg or 1 yolk
5 oz (125 g) self raising flour
½–1 teaspoon vanilla essence
1–1½ Weetabix
10–12 glacé cherries

Use the double-bladed knife. Place the chopped up lard and butter or margarine in the bowl with the sugar, whisked egg or yolk, flour and vanilla essence and process for 10 seconds, stop and stir down then process for another 5 seconds until blended. Crumble the Weetabix onto a large plate. Take small teaspoonsfuls of the mixture, roll into balls and coat in the Weetabix. Place apart on a greased baking sheet, flatten the balls and press a quarter of a cherry into the centre of each. Bake in a moderately hot oven (375°F/190°C/Gas 5) for about 15–20 minutes. Cool on a rack and store in a tin or freeze.

Banana Milk Shake

If you feel like offering a milk drink as well as or instead of fruit juice, then this milk shake with banana and strawberry ice cream is very popular. It's also easy for children to whip up for themselves on a hot day.

1 very generous milk shake
8 fl oz (225 ml) milk
1 banana
1 scoop strawberry ice cream

Use the double-bladed knife. Place the roughly cut up banana in the Magimix bowl, process for about 15 seconds until almost smooth then add a scoop of ice cream. Process again and, once smooth and with the motor still running, pour in the milk. You can use up to 12 fl oz (350 ml) milk with 1 large banana and 2 scoops ice cream which will make approx 18 fl oz (550 ml) or 3 × 6 fl oz (200 ml) servings. Switch off and pour at once (or the liquid may find its way down the central column) into a tall glass or jug. Keep in the fridge (for not longer than 2–3 hours) if not using at once.

Coloured straws with the Banana Milk Shake are pretty

Fresh Fruit Jellies

To keep as close as possible to the colour scheme, I like to make pink, green and yellow jellies. Yellow is best made with water and with a little dice of apple and orange. Red jellies made as a milk jelly give a good, if rather lurid pink into which I slice banana; and green can either be made with water, or with a small proportion of milk to match up with icing and balloons etc, and with grapes and apple added. All milk jellies must be made with great care and the jelly must be absolutely cold, or setting before milk is added. If you use little waxed paper jelly dishes, they will hold about 3 fl oz (75 ml) of jelly each, so each 1 pint (600 ml) of jelly will fill 6–7 moulds.

6–7 jellies of each colour

Pink

1 packet red jelly
4 fl oz (100 ml) boiling water
12 fl oz (350 ml) milk
1 banana

Yellow

1 packet yellow jelly
10 fl oz (300 ml) boiling water
6 fl oz (175 ml) cold water or ice cubes
½–1 apple
1 orange

Green

1 packet green jelly
8 fl oz (225 ml) boiling water
3 fl oz (100 ml) cold water or ice cubes
5 fl oz (150 ml) milk
small handful green grapes
½ green apple

Pink. Dissolve the cubed jelly in the boiling water (I always do this in a saucepan so I can heat it if the jelly does not dissolve in this small amount of water). Once dissolved, leave the jelly to get absolutely cold or even set. Slice the banana and divide between the dishes.

Use the double-bladed knife. Turn the jelly into the Magimix bowl, process and add the milk gradually. Pour over the banana in the jelly dishes and leave to set.

Yellow. Dissolve the cubed jelly in the boiling water, turn into a measuring jug and add cold water or ice cubes to bring the level up to the 1 pint (600 ml) mark. Dice the apple and cut the peel, pith and skin from the orange. Remove the segments of flesh from the orange and dice. Divide between the jelly dishes. Once the ice has melted, pour the jelly over the fruit and leave to set.

Green. Dissolve the cubed jelly in the boiling water, turn into a measuring jug and add cold water or ice cubes to come up to the 15 fl oz (450 ml) level. Leave until absolutely cold or even set. Halve and de-pip the grapes, dice the apple and distribute between the jelly dishes.

Use the double-bladed knife. Turn into the Magimix bowl and process, adding the milk gradually. Pour over the fruit in the dishes and leave to set.

Use throw-away waxed paper dishes for the jellies

A Teenage Hop or Barbecue

———— ◆ ————

Teenage children like to have very informal, relaxed and preferably rather unusual parties. They are old enough to have got beyond being dressed up in mum's idea of party best but, as it would be BORING to wear everyday clothes, an element of dressing up, fancy dress and even fantasy usually creeps in. They like a party to have a theme; everyone wears a sequined mask or dresses only in scarlet and gold or are castaways or it's a Beggars' Ball. Oxfam shops are ransacked, hair is stiffened into odd coxcombs with egg-white or sprayed with rainbow colours, make up is allowed and liberally applied (by both sexes) to create the up to the minute fantasy of their imagination; behind all this, of course, lurk shy but emerging teenagers, the façade allowing them the licence to come out of their shell and relax. If it's only an informal barbecue, out come all the oldest and most disreputable of their clothes; jeans you had thought safe in the dustbin months ago, reappear, cut off and carefully ragged at the knees. Ancient T-shirts are snipped into (or out of) shape; a hole is cut to display a navel, they're worn one top of each other and begaudied with paint and glitter – anything for that stunning, parent-boggling effect that satisfies the teenager more than anything else! I love it and am continually amazed at the ingenuity they show to produce an often startling effect, sometimes unbelievably awful but always showing a non-conformity and a desire to be treated as individuals.

Funnily enough (and perhaps I shouldn't mention it in a cookery book!) food is less important at this sort of party than the music, the lights and what there is to drink. Life is so exciting and they are in such a hurry, with so many people to meet and so much gossip to exchange, that there's hardly time to eat. Food is something to be grabbed *en passant*, something you can pick up in your fingers and dash off with. So what I aim at is a buffet, laid out with what I might describe as stylish fast food (much of which can be made by the teenagers), and so positioned that they don't need to go looking for it (as a parent, I'm keen that they don't live it up on an empty stomach). Things like Home Made Sausage Rolls, Koftas on Sticks, Pizza Portions, little Triple Decker Sandwiches and, most popular of all, Fresh Vegetables and Mayonnaise Dips. Fruit goes down well and so do chocolate Eclairs or Profiteroles and individual puddings like Chocolate and Raspberry Mousse. As the buzz goes round that the food's not all that bad, so the interest in it increases.

A barbecue can augment or take the place of the buffet. Everyone enjoys cooking their own food and the welcome of the fire makes a gathering place for any who are slightly lost. It's essential to have someone you can trust on the barbecue; the teenagers aren't very good because their interest wanders and so do they. I usually try to persuade a friendly father or a bachelor who needs a square meal to do it for me. The smell of barbecuing sausages, Home Made Sausage Burgers or Spicy Chicken Drumsticks wafts up and reminds dancers how hungry they are and fresh rolls will soon fill up those who are at the 'eat a horse' stage. The barbecue needs to be big enough and we usually rig up a Heath Robinson arrangement of a rigid grid we happen to have, covered with wire netting with a mesh small enough to avoid incinerating too many sausages and set on bricks – inelegant but quite effective. It needs lighting early enough as it always takes longer to get to the really hot ember stage than one thinks, and nothing is more boring than perfectly cooked drum-sticks half an hour after the end of the party. Whoever is in charge needs good scissor tongs, a

M E N U

Buffet

Pizza Portions

Herby Cheese Turnovers

Home Made Sausage Rolls

Koftas on Sticks (page 74)

Triple Decker Sandwiches

Fresh Vegetables and Mayonnaise Dips

————

Eclairs or Profiteroles

Magimix Hot Chocolate Sauce

Chocolate Orange Mousse (page 63)

Strawberry or Raspberry Mousse (page 26)

Fresh Fruit (no recipe)

————

Drinks

Orange Apple Fizz

Barbecue

Sausages (no recipe)

Home Made Sausage Burgers

Spicy Chicken Drumsticks

Barbecue Sauce

Magimix Brown Rolls (page 115)

Nicola gives a barbecue party for her daughter and some friends

couple of kitchen forks, a brush with which to paint oil on the chicken, the reflective temperament of a Buddhist monk, the ability to squat for hours on end, the patience of Job and asbestos fingers! It's no good expecting everyone to queue when the sausages are *à point*; they will be gyrating to (and with) the current Number 1 or dashing round the garden. So it is handy to have one end of the barbecue rather cooler than the other where cooked food can be stacked until the spirit moves them to come and eat. Paper plates, paper napkins and plastic knives that don't need washing, seem to fit the general scene and end up cheaper than using your best china.

What you give them to drink depends on the age group. They seem to prefer walking about with a can, be it beer or coke, instead of a glass. Big party cans are cheaper, of course, and we find a good drink is Orange Apple Fizz, non-alcoholic, very refreshing and popular (as a change) even with hardened beer drinkers. It's less muddling if cup drinks like that are non-alcoholic because then everyone knows where they are and they don't overdo it. If you are offering wine, which is certainly very popular, while probably choosing nothing too expensive, give some thought to the alcoholic strength; something like a light Moselblumchen exactly fits the bill, not too dry, refreshing but relatively low in alcohol.

However bizarre the teenagers look, however frenetic their movement, whatever attitudes they adopt, they are real people, great communicators who can talk to other generations, older or younger and they will appreciate and thank you for all the trouble you take to give them a good party.

Pizza Portions

Inexpensive, easy to make and always popular. Pizza is ideal for a teenage party and pretty popular at any time. This is a large oblong version which will fit the oven and which can be cut into squares, cubes or fingers, depending on how you want to eat it. It also freezes well, only needing re-heating.

Pizza Dough

1 lb (450 g) strong white bread flour
3 oz (75 g) margarine
1 oz (25 g) fresh yeast or 1 packet Harvest Gold dried yeast
1 egg
7 fl oz (200 ml) milk and water mixed
1 teaspoon salt

Pizza Topping

2 onions
4–6 tablespoons olive oil
6 oz (175 g) mushrooms
2 × 14 oz (400 g) tins tomatoes
3–4 tablespoons tomato purée
2 cloves garlic
1 teaspoon cornflour
2 teaspoons dried oregano
salt and pepper

To Decorate

8 oz (225 g) cheddar cheese
1 tin anchovies
a few black olives
a few slices salami   } some or all
a few prawns   of these
sliced red or green pepper
oregano

Pizza portions

Pizza Dough. *Use the double-bladed knife or dough dome and plastic dough blade.* Place flour, salt, yeast and chopped up margarine in the Magimix bowl and process to rub in the margarine. Mix warm water and milk to make a tepid liquid. Whisk the egg and add to the liquid then, with the machine running, pour it down the tube and once the mixture has formed into a dough, process for 30 seconds. Turn the dough into a large bowl with a few drops of oil in the bottom. Turn the dough round in the oil and flip it over so the oily side is uppermost. Cover with a plastic bag and leave in a warm place for about 1 hour or until doubled in bulk.

Pizza Topping. *Use the standard slicing disc.* Cut the onions in quarters and slice. Heat the oil in a large frying pan and cook the onions until golden. Stack the mushrooms carefully in the feed tube and slice; add to the pan and fry for several minutes. Now add the chopped garlic, roughly chopped tomatoes and their juice (I just cut backwards and forwards in the tin with a knife), the tomato purée and oregano to the frying pan and season. Simmer down for about 30 minutes to a rich tasting sauce, add the cornflour, mixed with a little cold water, and boil for several minutes to thicken.

Knead the dough briefly then divide into two. Roll each piece to fit a swiss roll or baking tin roughly 10 × 14 in. (25 × 35 cm). Slip inside a plastic bag and again leave to rise in a nice warm place for 10–20 minutes until a little puffed up.

Use the fine grating disc. Grate the cheese. Carefully spoon the tomato pizza topping onto the dough and spread to the edges; decorate with olives and anchovies (or salami, prawns or peppers) and sprinkle with the cheese. Scatter a few pinches of oregano on top. Leave to rise for a little longer until looking nicely puffed, then cook in a hot oven (425°F/220°C/Gas 7) for about 15–20 minutes until the cheese is melted and bubbling and the bread cooked. Do not overbrown or overcook the bread base for it can get rather dry.

Cut each tin into portions; you will get 36 finger portions out of each tin or you can cut it into larger squares. There should be enough as a main course for 8 hungry teenagers!

It can be cooked ahead and rewarmed when ready to serve, for pizza portions are nicest served warm.

Herby Cheese Turnovers

Little triangles of rough puff pastry, filled with a herby or spicy cheese filling, are a bit of a fiddle to make but can all be prepared and frozen ready to cook. They are best served piping hot though they can be served cold or rewarmed successfully. They are very good for drinks parties, picnics and snacks as well as being popular at teenage parties.

20 turnovers

Rough Puff Pastry

8 oz (225 g) plain flour
2 oz (50 g) firm chilled butter
2 oz (50 g) chilled lard
6–7 tablespoons iced water
½ teaspoon salt

Cheese Filling

4 oz (100 g) cheese (cheddar, sage derby, double
    gloucester or cheese with herbs and garlic)
½ oz (12 g) butter
1 finely chopped onion
1 small egg
plenty of scissored chives and a few sprigs of lemon
    thyme or thyme or ½ teaspoon dried mixed herbs
several dashes of tobasco sauce or ¼ teaspoon chilli
    powder
salt and pepper

The Rough Puff Pastry being made, rolled out and filled for the Herby Cheese Turnovers

Rough Puff Pastry. Cut the butter and lard into little fingernail sized cubes and chill well; a few moments in the freezer is a good idea.

Use the double-bladed knife. Place the flour and salt in the Magimix bowl and process for several seconds to 'sift'. Have the measured water ready then add the chilled butter and lard cubes. Switch on and pour the water down the tube and switch off the moment the pastry draws together and while the fats are still in pea-sized bits. Turn onto a floured board, knead briefly together and roll to a roughly 9 × 5 in. (24 × 13 cm) rectangle. Brush off excess flour and turn the top third down and the bottom third up; press the edges together, turn a quarter turn clockwise and roll and fold once more. Pop in a plastic bag to rest in the fridge for ½–2 hours or freeze for future use.

Cheese Filling. *Use the double-bladed knife.* Soften the finely chopped onion in butter. Place in the Magimix bowl with crumbled cheese, herbs and plenty of seasoning; process until chopped then add the egg and process until creamed. Roll the pastry thinly to a rectangle, at least 12 × 15 in. (32 × 40 cm) and cut into 3 in. (8 cm) squares. Place a teaspoonful of the herby cheese on each square of pastry, moisten the edges with water and fold over to form a triangle; seal the edges carefully and cut a little slit in the top of each. Place on a greased baking sheet and bake in a hot oven (425°F/220°C/Gas 7) for 10 minutes then turn down to moderately hot (375°F/190°C/Gas 5) and continue to cook for about 10 minutes until puffed and pale golden.

Crisp and golden Herby Cheese Turnovers

Home Made Sausage Rolls

By using the home made sausagemeat, as made for the Sausage Burgers, you can have really meaty sausage rolls. You can make them with Rough Puff Pastry or with bought puff pastry. If you use Saxby's fresh puff pastry, you can prepare them all then freeze them ready to cook.

24 sausage rolls
1 batch Rough Puff Pastry (page 99) or
    1 lb (450 g) ready made puff pastry
⅓ batch home made Sausage Burger (page 104) or
    1 lb (450 g) sausagemeat
egg wash

Process the Sausage Burger meat until it is really smooth for these.

Roll the pastry out to ¹⁄₁₆ in. (2 mm) thickness and about 10 × 24 in. (25 × 60 cm) in size then cut it in half lengthways. Divide the sausagemeat into two and form into two long sausages, the length of the pastry. Lay these in place on the pastry so you can fold the pastry over to encase the sausagemeat; fold it over; moisten the edges with cold water and seal. Cut each length into 12 equal sized sausage rolls. Brush with egg wash and bake in a hot oven (425°F/220°C/Gas 7) for 10–15 minutes until the pastry is crisp and brown underneath as well as on top and the sausagemeat cooked. Preferably serve hot.

Triple Decker Sandwiches

Triple Decker Sandwiches

Nothing beats really good fresh sandwiches. I like to cream the butter in the Magimix, for easy spreading is half the secret of good sandwiches. The other essentials are really fresh bread and generous fillings.

Whilst creaming the butter in the Magimix, I introduce various flavourings, depending on what the filling will be. These flavoured butters not only taste good, but they speed up the time it takes to make a large quantity of sandwiches. This is a trick I discovered when we used to cater for weddings and parties. With smoked salmon, I cream pepper and lemon juice into the butter; with beef I use Béarnaise Butter or add horseradish to the creamed and seasoned butter. Watercress or cress butter is delicious and so pretty, but it must be used fresh. With ham, I use this Mustard Butter. By making triple decker sandwiches, then cutting them into tiny triangles to serve on plates or impaled on cocktail sticks, you make something appetising, attractive and easy to eat.

9 slices very fresh brown sliced bread
9 slices very fresh white sliced bread
6 slices ham

Mustard Butter
3 oz (75 g) soft butter
1 tablespoon dijon mustard
pinch tarragon
2–3 tablespoons cream

Cress Butter
4 oz (100 g) soft butter
1 box cress
1 lemon
salt and pepper

Mustard Butter. *Use the double-bladed knife.* Cream the soft butter until very soft; then add mustard and tarragon and process whilst dripping in the cream. Set aside.
Cress Butter. *Use the double-bladed knife.* Cream the soft butter until very well creamed, then add scissored cress and seasoning; process until smooth and green, dripping in lemon juice to taste.

Use very fresh bread. Pile the bread up and cut the crusts off with a very sharp knife. Lay 3 brown and 3 white slices on a damp tea towel; spread them all with mustard butter and lay a slice of ham on each.

Now spread 3 more brown and 3 more white slices with the remaining mustard butter and lay, buttered side down, brown on white slice and white on brown slice, on top of the ham. Spread the top of these slices with generous quantities of cress butter and top with remaining slices of bread, brown on white. Press together, stack the sandwiches and quickly wrap in cling-film to keep really fresh.

When ready to serve, cut the pile of triple deckers into four diagonally and cut each pile in half again to make really small sandwiches. Serve on a plate (keep covered with damp tea towels or cling-film until about to be eaten) or spike onto cocktail sticks if you wish.

———————— : ————————

Fresh Vegetables and Mayonnaise Dips

Strips of crunchy fresh vegetables with a few twiglets and crisps, seem to be one of the great favourites of the young. Sticks of carrot, celery, pepper and cucumber or knobbly lumps of cauliflower are hastily plunged into a dipping sauce and pelicanned down.

They are so easy to prepare, quick to replenish and look so good laid out on cabbage leaves on a wide basket and decorated with vegetables. A bowl of Magimix Mayonnaise, Curried or Avocado Dip is set in the middle.

1 cucumber
1 head celery
bunch carrots
1 red pepper ⎫
1 green pepper ⎭ optional
1 cauliflower
a few young courgettes
1 box twiglets
large packet crisps

Magimix Mayonnaise
1 egg or 2 yolks
1 teaspoon dijon mustard
2 teaspoons wine vinegar
½ pint (300 ml) mixed olive and light vegetable oil
salt and pepper

Wash and prepare all the vegetables and cut into long strips or florets. Arrange in piles on a large dish with the bowl of dip in the centre.

Magimix Mayonnaise. *Use the double-bladed knife.* Place the whole egg or yolks in the bowl with the mustard, salt, pepper and 1 teaspoon vinegar. Process for 15–20 seconds then gradually add the oil, in a fine trickle to start with and then a little faster. When the mixture 'takes' and begins to 'slurp-slurp', add the oil more quickly (especially to the yolks only variety). Do not dwell on it or your mayonnaise will become thick and white, too tightly emulsified and quite unlike hand-made mayonnaise. Once made, stir down, correct seasoning (mayonnaise needs plenty of salt), adjust vinegar and use or keep for up to 10 days in the fridge (never stir vigorously straight from the fridge or it may curdle; allow to come to room temperature first). Turn into a bowl to serve with the vegetables.

Variations
Curried Dip. To the mayonnaise above, add 2–3 tablespoons tomato ketchup, 1–2 teaspoons curry paste and a good squeeze of lemon juice. Mix or process together.

Avocado Dip. *Use the double-bladed knife.* Scrape the flesh from 2 avocadoes into the Magimix and process until smooth, adding the juice of 1–2 lemons; then add in ½ pint (300 ml) Magimix mayonnaise and process together.

Eclairs or Profiteroles

Mouthfuls of choux pastry, filled with cream and topped with chocolate, are hard to resist at any time but after a strenuous bout of disco dancing, they slip down remarkably easily.

You can use the choux pastry to make finger éclairs, filled with cream and chocolate iced, or cook the choux mixture in round buns, which are then filled with cream and served, 3–4 in a bowl, with the marvellous Magimix Hot Chocolate Sauce. They make a wonderful dinner party pudding and the sauce is also superb with ice cream.

30–40 éclairs or profiteroles
Choux Pastry
3 fl oz (75 ml) water
3 fl oz (75 ml) milk
3 oz (75 g) butter
½ teaspoon salt
scant 4 oz (100 g) strong white bread flour, sifted
3 eggs

Filling
12–15 fl oz (350–450 ml) whipping cream
1–2 tablespoons vanilla sugar or to taste or
      castor sugar and vanilla essence

Putting the hot choux pastry dough into the Magimix

Filling the piping bag is easy if it is hung in a jug

To avoid the problem of dripping push end of bag into nozzle

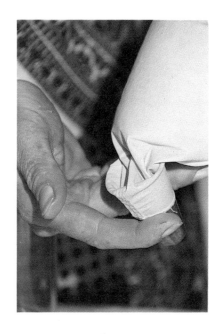

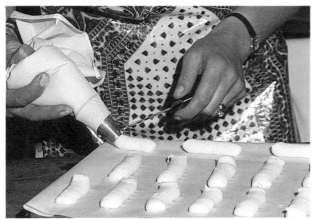

The Eclairs being piped onto a baking sheet. Cutting them off with a knife makes them tidier

Icing the Eclairs by dipping the top into a bowl of melted chocolate

Chocolate Icing for Eclairs
4 oz (100 g) plain eating chocolate like Bournville
1½ oz (35 g) lightly salted butter

Choux Pastry. *Use the double-bladed knife.* Place the chopped up butter, salt, milk and water in a saucepan and bring to the boil (the butter should melt before the liquid boils). Draw off the stove, tip in all the sifted flour and stir until a ball of dough forms; return to the stove and cook over moderate heat for 1–2 minutes, stirring until a skin forms on the bottom of the pan. Remove from the heat and turn into the Magimix bowl, spread round and leave to cool for 5 minutes. Start the motor, add the eggs one at a time down the tube and continue processing for 30–45 seconds until the mixture is smooth and shiny. Preferably leave the mixture to cool before baking. Pipe the mixture into 2 in. (5 cm) lengths for finger éclairs or place teaspoons of the mixture, well apart, onto an oiled baking sheet. Cook in a hot oven (425°F/220°C/Gas 7) for 10–15 minutes; turn down to moderately hot (375°F/190°C/Gas 5) and continue cooking, with the door open a crack, for 10 minutes or more until golden brown and crisp. Do not open the door wide or remove the buns until set and crisp or they may collapse. Make a small slit in each with a knife and leave in a cool oven for a few minutes to get rid of the steam. When cold, split and fill.

Filling. *Use the double-bladed knife.* Place the cream and vanilla sugar in the Magimix and process for about 20 seconds until thick (do not over-process and turn to butter!) Spoon into a piping bag with a plain nozzle and fill the éclairs or buns. (You can just spoon in the cream but it's quicker and easier, especially with small buns, to use a piping bag).

Eclairs are iced with the Chocolate Icing; dip the top of each éclair into the icing and leave on a rack to dry.

Profiteroles are served piled in a bowl, sprinkled with icing sugar and with Magimix Hot Chocolate Sauce, served hot, either handed separately or poured over the mound of profiteroles at the moment of service.

Chocolate Icing. Place the broken chocolate and butter in a bowl over hot water and stir until melted and it has become a smooth and shiny icing. Use at once.

Finger Eclairs are easy to eat and always popular

Magimix Hot Chocolate Sauce

One of the quickest, easiest and best chocolate sauces I have come across. Everything is processed together in the Magimix, then simmered gently until thick and rich.

4 oz (100 g) plain eating chocolate like Bournville
2 tablespoons golden syrup
1 tablespoon cocoa
½ oz (12 g) butter
½ teaspoon cornflour
½ teaspoon powdered coffee
¼ teaspoon vanilla essence
½ pint (300 ml) boiling water

Use the coarse grating disc. Grate the chocolate into the Magimix bowl.
Change to the double-bladed knife. Add all the remaining ingredients and process until smooth. Turn into a saucepan and bring to the simmer, stirring. Simmer very gently for about 15–20 minutes until thick and rich. Cover and keep warm until ready to use.

Home Made Sausage Burgers

Home made sausage meat is absolutely delicious. It's meaty, tasty and is without all that rusk filling that most commercial sausagemeat contains. Putting the mixture into sausage skins is rather a job but I find the sausage meat pats into excellent sausage burgers or can be rolled into sausage shapes or used in sausage rolls.

Back pork fat and seasoning are the secrets. Ask your butcher for fat from the back of the pig; it doesn't just melt and run out but keeps the sausage burgers moist and succulent. Pigs are bred so lean these days that you may have to give the butcher some notice so he can get it from a fat porker.

14 × 4 oz (100 g) or 18 × 3 oz (75 g) sausage burgers
2 lb (900 g) lean pork (from the shoulder)
1 lb (450 g) back pork fat
4 teaspoons salt
¼ teaspoon each ground allspice, ground cloves and
   nutmeg
1 teaspoon freshly ground black pepper
2 tablespoons fresh chopped parsley
1 tablespoon dried basil, sage, marjoram or thyme
4 oz (100 g) crustless bread (optional)
2 eggs

Cube the meat and fat, removing any skin, stringy bits and gristle. Sprinkle with the herbs, spices and seasoning and mix together well.

Break the eggs into a bowl and whisk lightly. *Use the double-bladed knife.* Process the bread (if used) into breadcrumbs and mix with the eggs.

Divide the meat and fat cubes into three piles. Switch on the Magimix and drop one pile down the feed tube onto the moving blades; process until finely chopped or smooth (depending what texture you like), adding some of the egg and breadcrumbs, then remove. Continue with the remaining batches and then combine and knead together with your hands. Wet your hands and form into 14 × 4 oz (100 g) or 18 × 3 oz (75 g) flattened discs or sausage burgers, about 4 in. (10 cm) diameter.

Cook on a hot barbecue or they can be fried in a little hot fat for about 5–6 minutes on each side or grilled. Slip into split, warmed soft rolls or Magimix Brown Rolls, made rather larger than usual. They can be served with fried onions or Barbecue Sauce.

Barbecue Sauce

Barbecue sauce is a must for teenagers. It is dolloped onto beefburgers or Sausage Burgers, Chicken Drumsticks are smothered in it and Koftas dipped in it. I leave a heavy casserole of it, with a ladle, keeping warm at the edge of the barbecue or stove. It just seems to get thicker and better.

2 onions
4 tablespoons oil
8 fl oz (225 ml) tomato ketchup
2 tablespoons worcester sauce
1–1½ tablespoons cornflour
5–6 tablespoons vinegar
4 tablespoons sugar
1 bay leaf

Use the double-bladed knife. Place the roughly cut up onions in the Magimix and chop finely with the on/off technique. Heat the oil in a casserole or pan and fry the onions a good golden colour.

Place all the other ingredients, except for the bay leaf, in the Magimix and process together. Add to the browned onions with the bay leaf. Simmer together gently for 10–15 minutes. Keep warm and serve with Sausage Burgers, Spiced Chicken Drumsticks or Koftas.

———— : ————

Spicy Chicken Drumsticks

Chicken drumsticks are marinated to make them juicy and tasty and then cooked on a barbecue until brown and crisp or oven roasted. They are good for nibbling in your fingers and are just what teenagers enjoy. For big parties, I cheat a bit and oven-cook the drumsticks until half done, then finish them over charcoal to achieve the sizzling, crispy barbecue effect. You can let them cool between oven cooking and the barbecue finish if this is easier.

15–20 drumsticks
15–20 chicken drumsticks
1½ tablespoons coarsely crushed sea salt
plenty of fresh ground black pepper

Marinade
8 fl oz (225 ml) olive or light oil
3 sprigs fresh or 1 teaspoon dried thyme
3 cloves garlic
1 tablespoon fresh or 1 teaspoon dried marjoram
2 sprigs rosemary
9–12 green peppercorns

Heat the oil in a saucepan.

Use the double-bladed knife. Place all the remaining marinade ingredients in the Magimix, switch on and pour in the hot oil but do not overchop. Leave to steep for an hour or so or overnight. I keep a bottle of this oil in the cupboard and use it to baste chops, steaks or chicken.

Pat the chicken drumsticks dry and rub generously with the flavouring oil; pour over any remaining oil and leave to marinate for several hours or overnight.

When ready to cook, remove from the oil and season *very* generously indeed with salt, preferably sea salt, and freshly ground pepper. Cook over charcoal, turning once or twice until crisp, brown and cooked.

You can also cook them in one layer on a rack in a roasting tin in a very hot oven (475°F/240°C/Gas 9) for about 25–30 minutes, basting with the oil, until cooked and brown. Sometimes I then dash them under a hot grill to help crispen the skin.

To pre-roast them prior to barbecuing, I would allow 20–25 minutes, depending on the number you are cooking at any one time.

Serve with fresh rolls and Barbecue Sauce if you wish.

Orange Apple Fizz

A light fruity drink with flavour and bubble but no alcohol – just the thing for when the disco pace gets furious. By having such an attractive drink, the alcohol consumption can be kept within bounds. The proportions are so easy; everything comes in litre containers that can be mixed quickly and correctly, however hectic or late it is. Platefuls of sliced cucumber, apple, orange or lemon, some cherries and a few sprigs of mint or borage, ready to pop in each glass, add a bit of style and provide something to nibble.

3 litres
1 litre chilled orange juice
1 litre chilled apple juice
1 litre chilled lemonade

To Decorate
sliced cucumber
sliced orange or lemon
sliced apple
cherries
sprigs mint or borage

Mix orange, apple and lemonade together in a large jug and add a few ice cubes. Pour into glasses and add sliced fruit and a sprig of mint or borage.

A choice is always appreciated and here we show the barbecue with Sausages, Spicy Chicken Drumsticks and Home Made Sausage Burgers

A Summer Picnic

⟡

I wish our climate was more reliable, for what is more romantic than one of those real, if elusive, picnics you see in pictures? You know, the ones where they have found an idyllic spot beside a perfect stream with neither horse-flies nor cow-pats, where the sun shines but it's not too hot and where the wind doesn't seem to be blowing a gale. Their wine is cooling in the river and won't slip its string

(which, boringly, they remembered to bring!) when they pull it out. Their whole salmon didn't break up in the boot of the car, no one sat on the strawberries and they found the place so easily. They did not go on and on round a succession of corners to find the spot that suited everybody and then ending up, with everyone in a bad temper, in a council tip! Yes, I love picnics but getting reality to comply with my vision is

---

M E N U	*Variations*
Fresh Salmon or Smoked Haddock Rillettes	**Prawn Stuffed Eggs** (page 57). Less expensive as a starter but, in this case, you would not want to serve the Potato and Garlic Cake or it would all end up a bit eggy.
Magimix Brown Rolls	**Red Pepper Soup** (page 28). A useful iced soup, ideal on a summer picnic.
———	
	Stuffed Pitta Bread. This is now easily obtainable in many places and can be filled with a variety of sliced fillings.
Cold Chicken Galantine	
Jellied Gaspacho Salad	———
Potato and Garlic Cake	**Turkey in Tarragon Mousseline Sauce** (page 130), **Chicken Liver Tartlettes** (page 15) or **Cold Marinated Pork** (page 46). All these would be nice alternatives to the Chicken Galantine.
———	**Tomato, Onion and Cheese Tart.** Just the thing for a picnic.
Strawberries or Raspberries and Cream (no recipe)	———
or	**Raspberry or Strawberry Mousse** (page 26). Use as an alternative when you can't get the fresh fruit.
Hazelnut and Raspberry Tart	———
	Potted Cheddar Cheese with Green Peppercorns and Cider (page 50). A good spreading cheese for picnics.

not easy. Find a perfect spot with lovely food and down comes the rain, or the site and the weather are perfect but the dog has eaten the chicken.

There are many time when a picnic seems a nice thing to do or is really the only possible option. It's so much cheaper to picnic when travelling than to go into a restaurant and it's the ideal lunch for a day in the country. You may need to take one to school sports day and it's a perfect start to a day at the races, at fashionable Henley or an evening of Mozart at Glyndebourne. But whether it's simple or exotic, certain criteria will always apply. First of all, the food must be appropriate to the occasion; by this I mean that an elaborate, decorated cold salmon and a glass of champagne suit Glyndebourne rather better than a windy Scots hillside. Secondly, it must look attractive, and this means when you come to eat it, not when you put it into the picnic basket; therefore you may have to rule out certain confections that won't travel and think seriously about the containers you use to transport it in. Thirdly, some of it will probably need to be kept cool (and perhaps some piping hot) because nothing is more depressing than the sight of runny pools of jellied salad, mayonnaise or butter lurking in the bottom of the hamper. Lastly, and this is a foible of ours with which you may not agree, I don't like too many rich, fatty things at lunchtime in the hot sun.

Nothing, especially if you've been walking or fishing all morning, is nicer than the simple picnic of really good sandwiches and a bottle of beer. You can have fresh baps filled with something like Chicken Liver Pâté or our Stuffed Pitta Bread; add a tomato, a wedge of good cheddar, a slice of fruit cake and a cup of coffee and what more could you want?

But, really, I'm talking more about the picnic where you say 'Let's lay out the tablecoth, unpack the hamper and uncork a bottle of wine'. As a starter, what about fresh Magimix Rolls, light brown with perhaps a hint of caraway, with Salmon or Smoked Haddock Rillettes? Should you go for Salmon Rillettes, you might follow it with the whole Chicken Galantine, perhaps with a Jellied Gaspacho Salad, served either in individual containers or scooped from a soufflé dish; this is colourful and does away with the need for bags of lettuce leaves, and a bottle of mixed vinaigratte; I for one always manage to let the lettuce leaves dangle off my plate, quietly trickling dressing into my lap or else wave it around

on the end of my fork, spattering everyone within reach. I must say, however, that a really good salad, carefully arranged in a large bowl and the whole enclosed in a plastic bag and carefully stowed with the dressing separate, is attractive and delicious. If you add a creamy new potato salad or my Potato and Garlic Cake, you've got something to fill up the hungry; you can vary this by adding chopped ham, shredded peppers, smoked sausage or anything of your choice to make it a complete main course for a simple picnic.

Alternatively, you may like the idea of a bowl of the Iced Red Pepper Soup to start with; I use one of those marvellous dispenser thermoses for this as it is essential to serve it really cold. In this case, it would be lovely to go on with classic cold salmon and mayonnaise and strawberries or raspberries and cream, perhaps with a slice of brie and a cup of coffee to gild the lily.

Another thing I find useful as a first course is a box of young carrot fingers, strips of florence fennel (if you like it), cucumber and celery – all nice and fresh and crunchy. Eat them plain with salt, with a dip or as an accompaniant to the main course to add colour to the plate. Quiches are always popular and often fit into the menu; the Tomato, Onion and Cheese Tart has no eggs so is not a true quiche but it's full of flavour.

Fresh strawberries or raspberries and cream are a perfect finish to a summer picnic or you can serve the Hazelnut and Raspberry Tart; this travels well but is not suitable to follow the Tomato, Onion and Cheese Tart.

A long, cool Pimms makes a good start after a hot drive or, as a non-alcoholic and absolutely delicious alternative try our own family favourite Orange Apple Fizz. White wine seems to suit the mood better than red and something light and fresh like Mosel, Soave or one of the delicious wines from Alsace will slip down very easily.

Like everything else, planning is the key to a successful picnic so that most of the preparation and packing can be done the day before or at least left ready in the fridge to pop into the coolbox, a great blessing if you have an early start. I've included a picnic check list to save you the annoyance of finding yourself in the most wonderful secluded spot, miles from anyone or anywhere, but quite unable to open the bottle!

Picnic Check List

Rugs, tablecloths (and something waterproof to go under them) or foldaway table and chairs (why be uncomfortable?).

Plates including plenty of serving dishes, baskets, etc. from which to serve the food (which looks horrid falling out of plastic bags).

Knives, forks and spoons including a sharp knife for cutting quiches etc, serving spoons, salad servers and teaspoons for the coffee.

Salt, pepper, a tube of mustard and your mixed vinaigrette or mayonnaise in a very well sealed jar.

Butter in an insulated container.

Sugar and milk or cream for fresh fruit and the coffee.

Thermos(es) for cold soup and/or hot coffee.

Glasses (people often use plastic but wine seems to taste better from glass).

Jugs.

Bottle opener and corkscrew.

Ice and fruit, borage mint etc. for Pimms.

Napkins, a roll of kitchen paper and a damp J cloth in a plastic bag (wonderful for spillages or sticky face and fingers).

Matches.

Polythene bags and fasteners (for dirty plates and cutlery, rubbish and perhaps for a doggy bag).

Fresh Salmon or Smoked Haddock Rillettes

I call this a rillettes because it is rough thready fish in a creamy mixture, not unlike the texture of true pork rillettes from Tours. It's utterly simple, and relies on the quality of the fish and is an inexpensive way of serving salmon. It makes a nice change from smooth pâtés, and is an excellent filling for Magimix Rolls with a little cress or as a starter or summer lunch dish with rolls, crisp bread or Brown Soda Scone and salad.

for 6–8 people
12 oz (350 g) salmon or smoked haddock
8 oz (225 g) cream cheese (Eden Vale Somerset soft cheese)
2–3 fl oz (75–100 ml) whipping cream
pinch of mace
salt and pepper

Place the fish in a roaster bag in a saucepan and cover with cold water; bring gently to the boil and then draw off the stove and leave for 5–10 minutes, by which time the fish will be cooked. Drain and cool, remove bones and skin and flake the fish roughly.

Use the plastic blade. It's important not to over-process the fish for it should not be too broken down or smooth. Place the flaked fish, cream cheese, mace and seasoning in the Magimix bowl and process with the on/off technique, adding in the cream, until you have a smooth, thready mixture. If the fish was warm (the best moment to do it), the mixture should be fairly soft; the cream cheese which softens with the heat from the fish, will firm up in the fridge as it cools. Correct seasoning and turn into a pot.

A roaster bag is good for preserving the salmon flavour but should not be used for salty smoked haddock

Chicken Galantine

A plump chicken, boned and stuffed with a light summer mixture of veal or pork and ham, rice and mushrooms sharpened with lemon juice, makes this a good cold summer dish. The chicken can be boned, stuffed, then poached in stock and left to cool. You will have a delicious succulent chicken and some wonderful stock as well. You can coat the chicken in aspic and decorate it, if you wish, but I frequently don't bother for the lemon slices, packed over the breast, keep it nice, white and attractive.

for 8–12 people
3½–4 lb (1.6–1.8 kg) chicken
2 oz (50 g) butter
1 onion
4 oz (100 g) button mushrooms
2 tablespoons dry white vermouth
12 oz (350 g) lean veal or pork
8 oz (225 g) back pork fat
4 oz (100 g) cooked ham
2 oz (50 g) rice boiled for 10 minutes and drained
2 eggs
1 lemon

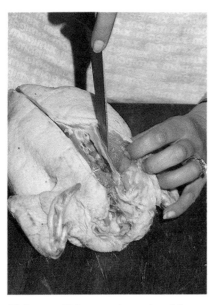

To bone a chicken start by cutting right down the backbone and then, one side at a time, gently ease off the flesh

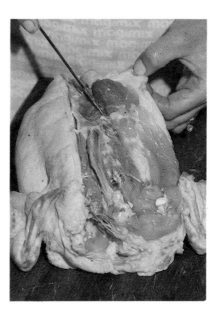

Keep your knife very close to the carcase and be careful not to pierce the skin

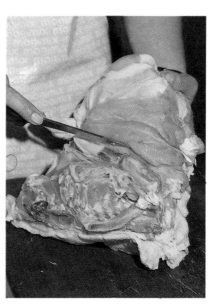

As you reach the wings and legs detach them from the carcase

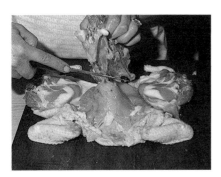

Remove the carcase

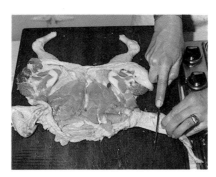

Cut off wings at the middle joint

From the inside remove the inner wing bone

handful of parsley heads, some marjoram, chives,
    summer savory or any fresh mixed herbs
sprig of fresh or ¼ teaspoon dried tarragon
2–3 tablespoons pistachio nuts (optional)
1–1½ teaspoon salt
plenty of pepper

Stock
the chicken carcase
1 onion
1 carrot
bouquet garni of parsley stalks, thyme and bay leaf
3 pints (1.7 l) light stock or water
salt and pepper

To bone out chicken cut right down the back with a
sharp knife; then gently ease skin and flesh off the
bone, working round to the front breastbone and
detaching wings and legs where they join the body.
Detach flesh from the breastbone very carefully so as
not to pierce the skin and lift out the chicken carcass.
Now cut the last two wing joints off and bone out the
remaining wing bone on each side, pulling the flesh
through to the inside. Remove the thigh bones but
leave the drumsticks. Make stock with the broken
carcase and the stock ingredients.

Use the double-bladed knife. Chop the parsley and
other herbs and set aside. Chop the roughly cut up
onion with the on/off technique until finely
chopped, then fry gently in the butter in a frying pan.
Change to the standard slicing disc. Pack the feed tube
carefully with mushrooms and slice. Add the
mushrooms to the onions and butter in the pan and
soften; then add the grated rind and juice of half the
lemon and the vermouth; cook to reduce the liquid
by half.
Change to the double-bladed knife. Cut the lean veal
or pork and back pork fat into cubes, remove all
gristle and mix together. Switch on the machine and
drop half the meat down the feed tube onto the
moving blades. Process until finely chopped, then
remove the minced meat before processing the rest.
Cut the ham into match-stick strips by hand for a
variation in texture (or process in with the meat and
fat if you wish).
Change to the plastic blade. Return all the meat to the
Magimix bowl together with the rice, onion-
mushroom mixture, parsley and herbs, tarragon,
eggs, seasoning and pistachio nuts, (if used). Process
well together and fry a bit to taste the seasoning; as it
is to be eaten cold it needs rather high seasoning, and
I always think it is worth frying a bit of the mixture to
get the seasoning just right.

Remove the thigh bone

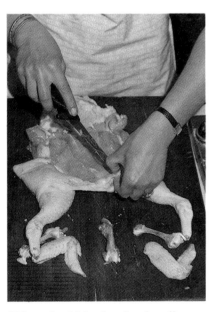

*Tidy up the chicken by trimming off any
excess fat*

The chicken boned and ready for stuffing

Lay the chicken skin side down on the table and mound the stuffing up well in the middle, making sure you get plenty between the chicken legs. Take a large darning needle and strong button thread and sew up the chicken, using large over-sewing stitches. Do not have the chicken too tightly stuffed for the skin shrinks tighter during cooking. Cover the chicken breast with wafer thin slices of lemon from the remaining half lemon, then roll the chicken up in a piece of butter muslin (an old piece of sheeting, or well perforated roaster bag) and tie each end so you have a firm sausage shape. Lower the parcel into the simmering stock and simmer until cooked (1½ –2 hours). Cool in the stock and un-parcel when cold. Decorate and coat with aspic if desired and serve cut in slices.

The stuffing is made altogether in the Magimix

The stuffing being spread onto the boned chicken

The chicken is sewn securely but not too tightly

The lemon slices add further flavour to the Galantine

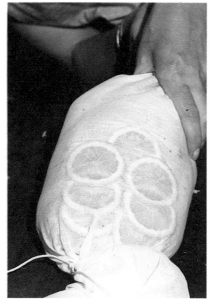

The wrapped up chicken is tied tightly at each end

The parcel is simmered gently in a light stock

This Galantine has been decorated and garnished for a very special picnic

The set Jellied Gazpacho Salads can be turned out and arranged attractively on a plate

Jellied Gazpacho Salad

The fresh flavours of tomato, cucumber, onion and pepper that make classic gazpacho soup are also excellent made into a salad, set with gelatine to a spooning consistency.

A Jellied Gazpacho Salad is the ideal way of eating fresh summer salad vegetables on a picnic

I like to eat this with yoghurt and a slice of Brown Soda Bread as a simple, healthful lunch as well as using it as an attractive and neat picnic dish.

for 6–8 people
1½ lb (675 g) tomatoes
1 cucumber
½–1 clove garlic
¼–½ mild spanish onion
1 green pepper
2 crustless slices brown bread
2 tablespoons wine vinegar
3 tablespoons olive oil
1 tablespoon gelatine
2–3 tablespoons cold water
salt and pepper

Use the double-bladed knife. Place the roughly torn bread in the Magimix and crumb; add the oil and vinegar and half the tomatoes and cucumber, roughly chopped, the garlic, the onion and half the green pepper, de-seeded. Process until very smooth and put through a sieve to remove pips and skin.

The grated cucumber being added to the salad

A further texture and bite is obtained by adding chopped green peppers

Sprinkle the gelatine onto the cold water in a small bowl, leave to soak for several minutes then stand the bowl in a pan of hot water to melt the gelatine. Then stir the melted gelatine into the gazpacho base.

Skin the remaining tomatoes, halve and remove seeds then dice up very small and add to the base mixture.

Use the coarse grating disc. Peel the remaining half cucumber, grate and add to the gazpacho.

Change to the double-bladed knife. Place the remaining roughly cut up green pepper in the Magimix bowl and process with the on/off technique until finely chopped; add to the gazpacho with a seasoning of salt and pepper. Turn into a 2 pints (1.2 l) bowl or eight individual 5 fl oz (150 ml) dishes and leave to set. Don't forget to oil the moulds lightly if you wish to turn the salad out, but for a picnic I just spoon it from the bowl.

———————— : ————————

Potato and Garlic Cake

A thick cake of sliced browned potatoes, onions, garlic and black olives, well flavoured with good olive oil. It can be cut in slices and is good to accompany the Chicken Galantine. It can also have all sorts of other bits and pieces added to it like cold meat, mushrooms, fried bacon or cheese; it then turns into a simple picnic main course and can just be served with a green or mixed salad.

for 6–8 people
2 lb (900 g) slightly undercooked boiled potatoes
5–6 tablespoons good olive oil
2–3 cloves garlic
1 large onion
8–10 black olives (optional)
4 eggs
a handful of herbs (chives, parsley, tarragon and chervil)
salt and pepper

Use the double-bladed knife. Place the roughly cut up onion and garlic cloves in the Magimix bowl and chop with the on/off technique until fairly finely chopped. Heat 4–5 tablespoons of the olive oil in a

heavy frying pan and gently fry the onion and garlic until softened and golden.

Change to the 6 mm slicing disc. Slice the cooked potatoes, but don't worry if they break up a bit. Add the potatoes to the oil and fry, turning from time to time, for 10–15 minutes so they brown in patches; add in the stoned and sliced olives if used.

Change to the double-bladed knife. Scissor the chives into the Magimix bowl and add plenty of parsley heads, some tarragon and some chervil or any fresh mixed herbs you may have. Chop the herbs, then break in the eggs, add seasoning and process until the herbs are more finely chopped and the eggs lightly beaten.

If the potatoes are sticking to the pan, remove and clean the pan with salt and kitchen paper (don't wash it or it will stick more), add the remaining oil to the pan and heat until almost smoking; then return the potatoes, pour over the eggs and pack down neatly. Now cook very gently on low heat for 15 minutes or so, with a lid on, until the egg has all set. Run a knife around the edge of the pan, put a plate over the potato cake then invert pan and plate so the cake comes out of the pan and onto the plate. It can be eaten hot but for picnics, leave until cold and cover closely. Serve cut into wedges.

———————— : ————————

Magimix Brown Rolls

These rolls are so quickly made in the Magimix; they are processed and formed without an initial rise and, by using a rather soft dough, they are none the worse for being made with such speed. With the dough dome, you can use 1½ lbs (675 g) flour in the Standard Magimix. But keep the dough firm enough, so it can freely roll around the bowl until it has been kneaded, then if necessary add the last of the liquid to make a softer dough.

24 rolls
12 oz (350 g) granary or wholemeal flour
12 oz (350 g) strong white bread flour
½ oz (12 g) butter, margarine, lard or oil
1½ oz (35 g) fresh or 1 packet Harvest Gold dried yeast
17 fl oz (500 ml) milk or milk and water mixed
2 teaspoons sea salt

Harvest Gold dried yeast can just be tipped into the bowl with the other ingredients; but the result is better with fresh yeast and the dough will usually rise more quickly.

Use the plastic dough blade. Place the flours, fat, crumbled yeast or dried yeast and the salt (remember that sea salt is less powerful than other salt so adjust if you use Cerebos or suchlike) into the Magimix bowl and process to mix. Mix hot water with cold milk to make a tepid mixture or if using all milk, warm it in a saucepan. Pour most or all of the liquid down the feed tube whilst processing, but keep the dough in one lump so that it can roll easily around the bowl and dome; once the mixture has drawn into a dough, continue to process for about 30 seconds. If you have any liquid left, add it only at the end to make the dough softer; too soft a dough initially can drag on the blades.

Turn the dough out onto a well floured board and sprinkle with flour; try not to work in any more flour

Crumbling the fresh yeast into the Magimix bowl

Pouring in the tepid milk and water while the Magimix is working

The consistency of the finished dough should be soft and pliable

The dough being gently kneaded into shape

It is quick and easy to cut the dough into triangular shapes

(These photographs show the large capacity Magimix 3500 Grande Famille rather than the Standard Magimix with the dough dome as described in the text: They will both knead dough made with 1½ lb of flour)

but keep it well cocooned in it. Knead into a smooth ball, roll into a fat sausage, divide into twenty-four even pieces and form into round or long rolls. (In real haste, I form each half of the dough into a long roll, flatten the top and cut it into 12 triangular pieces). Place the rolls on a greased baking sheet and slip them inside a large polythene bag so they are in a moist, warm atmosphere (put a few drops of oil inside the bag and rub it around so the polythene won't stick if it should touch the dough). Another ploy is to blow up the polythene bag like a balloon and seal it so the rolls are safe inside a polythene balloon bag. Leave in a warm place until double in size; this usually takes from ¾–1½ hours, depending on warmth and dried yeast taking appreciably longer then fresh. I find most people do not let bread rise enough. Then cook in a hot oven (425°F/220°C/ Gas 7) for 10–15 minutes until brown and cooked. Cool on a rack, under a cloth if you want soft rolls.

————— : —————

Hazelnut and Raspberry Tart

A pastry case with a generous layer of raspberry jam is topped with a spongy meringue, coffee and nut layer and baked to make a delicious tart, lovely to take on a picnic but just as good on any other occasion. You can ice it with a little rum icing and scatter it with flaked hazelnuts, but I'm not sure that isn't gilding the lily a bit!

for 6–8 people
Pastry
6 oz (175 g) plain flour
4 oz (100 g) firm butter
2 tablespoons icing sugar
1 egg yolk
1–2 tablespoons iced water
a pinch of salt

Filling
5–6 tablespoons raspberry jam
3 eggs
4 oz (100 g) castor sugar
2½ oz (60 g) walnuts ⎫ or use all
2½ oz (60 g) hazelnuts ⎭ hazelnuts

2 teaspoons powdered coffee
1 tablespoon rum

Pastry. *Use the double-bladed knife.* Place the flour, icing sugar and salt in the Magimix bowl and add the butter, cut up into hazelnut sized pieces. Process to the breadcrumb stage. With the motor still running, add the egg yolk mixed with cold water but switch off as the mixture combines into one lump. Turn onto a floured board and knead briefly into a flat disc before resting in the fridge for ½–2 hours. Roll and line a 9 in. (24 cm) tart tin. Prick the base and cover with a generous layer of raspberry jam. Spoon over the filling and bake in a moderately hot oven (375°F/190°C/Gas 5) for 40–50 minutes until golden and the pastry is cooked. Cool on a wire rack. Serve hot, warm or cold.

Filling. *Use the double-bladed knife.* Process the hazelnuts and walnuts until finely ground. Set aside.

Separate the eggs and process the yolks in the Magimix with the sugar until pale and thick. Add the nuts, rum and coffee powder and process again. The mixture will be a firm paste at this stage. Whisk the egg whites until just holding a peak and add a spoonful to the mixture; process briefly, using the on/off technique, until the egg white is incorporated and the mixture slacker. Now add the remaining egg white and process very briefly again using the on/off technique, stopping to stir round with a spatula, until the two mixtures are just combined. Use at once.

For a grand picnic the Hazelnut and Raspberry Tart is delicious on a plate with a dollop of whipped cream

The Magimix is wonderful for thin slices of cucumber which give a lovely fresh taste to the Stuffed Pitta Bread

The shredded lettuce being added to the bowl of grated cheese, onion, carrots and chopped herbs

Stuffing the salad mixture into the Pitta Bread

Stuffed Pitta Bread

These middle eastern breads, split and stuffed to make a bulging pocket, are ideal for the simple sort of picnic or day out when everyone is given their own packet to eat as and when they like. Children, like the proverbial soldier, often prefer to carry their haversack ration safe in their tummy and surreptitious unwrapping and nibbling goes on soon after rations have been issued!

Many different things can be packed inside the pitta bread. Kebabs are the classic and arguably the best; but you might try Koftas or just chopped cold chicken, meat or hard boiled eggs, added to seasonally varying salad ingredients.

for 6–8 people
6–8 pitta breads
½ lb (225 g) sliced garlic sausage or salami
½ cucumber
6–8 oz (175–225 g) cheddar cheese
3–4 carrots
½–¾ crisp iceburg lettuce or chinese leaves
3–4 tomatoes
1 sweet onion or some spring onions
handful parsley or fresh coriander heads
3–4 tablespoons mayonnaise
a few anchovy fillets } optional
a few stoned black olives }
salt and pepper

Use the standard slicing disc. Slice the cucumber and set aside.
Use the double-bladed knife. Chop the parsley or coriander and put into a large bowl.
Use the coleslaw or coarse grating disc. Grate the cheese, onion and carrots and combine in the bowl with the chopped parsley or coriander and the lettuce, shredded not to finely with a knife. Season and mix all together with a little mayonnaise but not too much or the pitta bread will become soggy. Add some chopped anchovy fillets and olives if you like them.

Slice the tomatoes by hand.

Warm the breads for a few moments, in the oven or under a low grill, so they can be split open easily. Cut an opening at the narrow end and slip your knife between the two layers of bread to form a pocket. Layer with sliced garlic sausage, cucumber and tomato then stuff with the shredded salad mix. Close up and wrap in cling film to keep fresh.

Tomato, Cheese and Onion Tart

Slow cooked onions and quick fried tomatoes combine to make this delicious tart. It is decorated with anchovies and olives and if it is to be eaten cold as a picnic dish scatter it with cheese, or if it is to be a hot main course smother it. Either way, it's a very tasty and popular tart. I use a really good all purpose pastry which is perfect for quiches and tarts.

4–6 as a main course
6–8 as a starter or picnic dish

All purpose pastry
6 oz (175 g) plain flour
3 oz (75 g) firm butter
1 egg yolk and about 2 tablespoons cold water or
    3–4 tablespoons cold water
a good pinch salt

Filling
1½ lb (675 g) onions
1½ oz (35 g) butter
1 lb (450 g) fresh or 1 × 14 oz (400 g) tin tomatoes
2–3 tablespoons olive oil
2 tablespoons tomato purée
1 teaspoon fresh or ¼ teaspoon dried chopped
    rosemary
1 tablespoon fresh or ½ teaspoon dried chopped basil
2 or 4 oz (50 or 100 g) mozarella or cheddar cheese
a few black olives and anchovy fillets to decorate
    (optional)
salt and pepper

Pastry. *Use the double-bladed knife.* Mix water with egg yolk if used. Place the flour and salt in the Magimix bowl and add the cubed butter; switch on and immediately pour the egg and water, or just water, down the tube; switch off as pastry draws into one lump. Remove and knead briefly into a smooth disc. Rest the pastry, wrapped, in the fridge for ½–1 hour before using it.

Roll the pastry thinly to fit a 9 in. (23 cm) flan tin; prick the pastry, line with tinfoil and baking beans and bake in a hot oven (400°F/200°C/Gas 6) for 6–8 minutes until the pastry has set. Remove the tinfoil and beans and continue to bake in a moderately hot oven (375°F/190°C/Gas 5) for a further 8–10 minutes until the crust is nearly cooked but not too brown. Spread with the tomato-onion mixture, scatter lightly or generously with cheese and decorate with anchovy fillets and black olives; sprinkle over a few pinches of basil and return to the oven to bake for 15–20 minutes. Serve hot, warm or cold.

Tomato and Onion Filling. *Use the 4 mm slicing disc.* Slice the onions and add to the melted butter in a frying pan. Cook gently for 30–40 minutes until soft and golden; season with salt, pepper and chopped rosemary and set aside. Peel, de-seed and slice the tomatoes (fresh ones can be sliced in the Magimix, tinned need only draining and rough chopping with a knife). Add the oil to the frying pan and, when hot, fry the tomato purée and tomatoes fairly fast until the liquid has evaporated and the mixture is quite stiff. Combine the two mixtures, season and add some of the basil.

Leave the Tomato, Cheese and Onion Tart in the flan dish for easy transportation

An Inexpensive and Easy Buffet Party

A buffet party for up to twenty five people which won't break the bank, or the hostess's back, is quite a tall order. It's one I used to hate being presented with but now, thank goodness, even the daunting thought of entertaining all these numbers can be faced with equanimity if you have a Magimix by your side.

Buffet parties may not be your favourite entertainment because who really enjoys balancing plate, knife and fork, glass and handbag while trying to carry on an intelligent conversation about Proust or the vagaries of your washing machine? Frequently, however, we are landed with them as the only way to entertain people we don't know well enough to have to dinner or it's a large family gathering and there isn't room to sit everyone down. Mind you, we shan't expect everyone to stand and can probably make provision for granny to find a comfortable seat; others will find themselves on groups of dining room chairs while the rest perch on the arms of sofas, on a cushion or form a coterie on the stairs. The important thing to remember is that the food must be easy to serve and to eat and, of course, look delicious and attractive. Try to avoid things that need cutting for brandishing a knife makes everything more difficult and dishes with too much gravy or sauce will be sure to spill and devastate your carpet. Everything should be able to be prepared well ahead and keep warm obligingly, so

M E N U	*Variations*
Spinach Velouté	**Vegetables in Sweet-Sour Ginger Dressing.** This is such a nice, fresh vegetable starter and would be good to precede either the Creamy Fish Pie or the cold turkey.
Fried Bread Croûtons or **Cheesy Herb Bread**	**Turkey in Tarragon Mousseline Sauce.** A very good cold buffet dish. It's probably best in summer when fresh tarragon is easier to find but not to be scorned with dried tarragon in winter.
Creamy Fish Pie and Puff Pastry Shapes	**Red Pepper and Green Bean Salad.** Lovely with the turkey and cheapest and best in summer.
Braised Carrot with Cumin	
	Strawberry or Raspbery Mousse (page 26). Very pretty on a buffet.
Wicked Chocolate Pudding	**Pineapple Tart.** Visually attractive and a bit of a crunch after creamy turkey. Other possible ideas are an orange or fresh fruit salad to add a bit of contrasting colour and freshness to your buffet.

I have prepared a relatively inexpensive menu, and some variations, that suits pretty well any time of year. The recipes are written for twelve so you can double them up for twenty five or halve them if you wish to use them for just a few people.

To help keep the price down, I am suggesting two vegetable starters. A simple spinach soup, delicate and comfortable, such as my grandmother's cook used to prepare but taking hours with the hair sieve in those days! This Spinach Velouté can be made ahead or frozen and is easy to serve. Soup is often the easiest hot dish to cope with if you have not got a lot of oven space or don't want to deal with a hot main course. My other suggestion is Vegetables in Sweet-Sour Ginger Dressing which is an unusual salad and the dressing is drawn from my experience of chinese food. This salad just cries out for some hot garlic bread or Cheesy Herb Bread to mop up the dressing.

If you like the idea of a hot middle course, here is a Creamy Fish Pie with a little bit of a difference. Instead of a pastry crust or potato topping, I prefer to serve Puff Pastry Shapes; these are cooked separately and so keep all their nice crisp crunchiness and, without a top, you can keep the fish carefully stirred to heat it evenly. You could use vol-au-vent shapes and fill them with some of the braised carrots but this is rather a last minute job. I would be inclined to cut the puff pastry into circles, squares, fingers or what you will; I know someone who cut it into letters and served it as Happy Birthday for her father's birthday. Carrots, braised gently in butter and stock and lightly seasoned with cumin, will reheat from cold, will keep warm easily and I find them a delicious match for the fish.

For a cold main course, turkey is always good value and of course is now available all the year round. I know it can sometimes be a little tasteless but if you poach it in our special way with flavouring vegetables and herbs, you will end up with plenty of taste, succulent meat and some wonderful rich stock with which to make the Tarragon Mousseline Sauce. The accompanying salad needs plenty of colour so I suggest a Red Pepper and Green Bean Salad which you could vary if you wish, by serving a plain green bean salad in a ring of Red Pepper and Lime Chartreuse.

I always think buffet puddings need to be specially attractive because they're all laid out and everyone can see them. My Wicked Chocolate Pudding can be made in as long a block as you have a suitable mould for and looks marvellous when decorated. Although it seems rather extravagant when you read the recipe, it is so rich that it really does go a long way and works out very reasonably. If you like a fruit pudding, Strawberry or Raspberry Mousse or Pineapple Tart are two of many that would look and taste the part.

A buffet party gives you the opportunity to present a good cheese board, showing a hard, medium soft and a cream cheese, with perhaps the Cheddar Cheese with Cider and Green Peppercorns as an inexpensive supplement. Some people even like to offer a fabulous cheese board and forget about puddings altogether.

On the whole, buffet parties cause peoples' imagination to wither and die on them and they return to the safety of dear old favourites time and time again. Don't be frightened to try something new. These are all attractive, easy dishes which are no great bother to prepare and which everyone will enjoy. I hope they will make your buffet party the success it deserves to be.

Spinach Velouté

By the time you have waited for everyone to arrive, some of your guests will have been drinking apéritifs for some time and the buffet will probably start quite late. This is a moment when people appreciate a good bowl of this warming soup to set them up for the evening. Add a little more interest with crisp Fried Bread Croûtons, easy to prepare ahead and serve and saving you the trouble of balancing a slice of bread on your saucer.

10–12 people

Spinach Base

1½–2 lb (675–900 g) fresh or 1 lb (450 g) frozen
    spinach
3 oz (75 g) butter
1 onion
2½ pints (1.5 l) chicken stock or 2 stock cubes
    (Knorr) and water
4 fl oz (100 ml) cream
salt and pepper

Bechamel Sauce

2 oz (50 g) butter
2 oz (50 g) plain flour
2 pints (1.2 l) milk
1 small onion
1 sprig rosemary
2 cloves
1 bayleaf
6 peppercorns
salt

Bechamel Sauce. Infuse the milk with the chopped onion, rosemary, cloves, bayleaf and peppercorns. Bring to the simmer, cover and leave by the side of the stove for 10–15 minutes.

Melt the butter in a large saucepan; the saucepan should be large enough to hold the finished soup and should not be aluminium which reacts with spinach, giving you that very teeth-edgy flavour. Add the flour and cook over a moderate heat for 3–4 minutes; draw the pan off the stove, wait for the sizzling to cease then add the infused milk through a strainer to catch the bits. Bring the sauce to the boil, whisking well and simmer for 1–2 minutes. Season lightly and set aside, covered, until ready to combine with the spinach.

Spinach Base. Wash the spinach well and tear off the tough stalks and midribs. Blanch in plenty of boiling salted water in a non-aluminium pan for 3–4 minutes, then drain and refresh under the cold tap. Squeeze out excess water with your hands and chop roughly. Frozen spinach only needs thawing and roughly chopping. Melt the butter in the saucepan, add the onion and soften gently before adding the spinach. Season lightly and cook, covered, until tender, stirring from time to time so the spinach does not catch and burn in the pan.

Use the double-bladed knife. Process the spinach, in two batches, in the Magimix until absolutely smooth then, with the machine still running, add some of the chicken stock. Pour the spinach mixture through a sieve into the prepared bechamel base. Whisk the two mixtures well together and add sufficient of the remaining chicken stock to thin the soup to your desired consistency. Re-heat, add the cream, correct the seasoning and serve with a bowl of Fried Bread Croûtons.

Adding fresh spinach to a pan of boiling water

Refreshing the cooked spinach under a cold tap helps to retain the colour

Fried Bread Croûtons

Do plenty while you're at it because they will keep in a box for a week or so and much longer in the freezer; they are so useful to shake out and reheat for soups, and in salads and omelettes.

The best flavour comes from using butter and olive oil to cook them; this is a bit extravagant for large quantities so I am often tempted to use the deep fryer. Keep the bread until it is nice and stale (4–5 days in the kitchen) so the croûtons are crisp and crunchy, not leathery as fried fresh bread tends to be.

for 10–12 people
10–12 slices stale white bread
2 oz (50 g) butter and 6 tablespoons oil (approx) for
  frying
or deep fat fryer

Take a very sharp knife and, letting the knife do the work (but don't squash the bread), cut the crusts off the piled slices of bread. Now cut the pile of slices across and across into little fingernail sized cubes. Heat the oil and butter in a frying pan until the frothing diminishes and before the butter burns, add some croûtons and toss and turn until golden brown. Drain from the hot fat, with a slotted spoon, onto kitchen paper and continue frying the rest. With a deep fryer, heat the oil until faintly hazing (390°F/200°C), add the croûtons to fry and remove and drain when golden brown.

These croûtons can be kept in a bag or box or in the freezer and only need reheating in a slow oven for 10–15 minutes.

Cheesy Herb Bread

This is a wow – everyone seems to go mad about it and it goes with the soup, if you don't want to do croûtons, or with the Vegetables in Sweet Sour Ginger Dressing. It can also be used as something hot to accompany a main course. As there is no garlic in it, it is far more use than the delicious, but rather anti-social, garlic bread.

1 loaf french bread
6 oz (175 g) butter
1½–2 teaspoons dried Italian seasoning
4 oz (100 g) cheddar cheese.

Chop up the butter, melt it in a small saucepan and add the italian seasoning.
Use the fine grating disc. Grate the cheese. Cut the bread in slanting slices but not quite through the bottom crust so it is still held together at the bottom. Lay the bread (you may have to halve it to fit it into your oven) on a piece of aluminium foil and using a pastry brush, preferably one marked 'garlic' and kept for this sort of task, paint both sides of each slice of bread with butter and herbs. Now put some grated cheese between each slice and close the foil up so that the loaf is parcelled. When ready to use, bake in a hot oven (425°F/220°C/Gas 7) for about 15 minutes until hot through and the cheese has melted. Fold back the top of the foil and serve the bread, sizzling hot, in the foil in a bread basket.

The butter and herbs being painted onto the 'half' sliced French bread

Adding the grated cheese before wrapping in foil and baking

Creamy Fish Pie and Puff Pastry Shapes

This can be made with just white and smoked fish and is a nice, everyday dish and very good value. Livened up with a few prawns and squid and possibly fresh mussels and scollops, you've got something really quite special. I know it has a lot of processses and would be too fiddly to do for four or five people, but it's well worth it for larger numbers. I have broken it up into the different processes, none of which are difficult, and I hope this will encourage you to try it. Don't be too British and avoid the squid which adds such a delicious flavour!

The puff pastry can be used in whatever shapes you like or cut into letters or dates to add a personal touch for a special occasion.

10–12 people
2 lb (900 g) cod or haddock fillet
1 lb (450 g) smoked haddock
¾ lb (350 g) prawns in their shells
½–¾ lb (225–350 g) small squid
3–4 scollops ⎫
1 lb (450 g) mussels ⎬ optional
3–4 hard boiled eggs (an optional extra to make it go further)
parsley to decorate

Prawn Butter
the prawn shells
5 oz (125 g) butter

Prawn Fumet
(this quantity will make enough for double the recipe and you can freeze any left over)
the prawn shells (having made prawn butter)
1–2 lb (450–900 g) extra white fish bones and skins (turbot and sole are best)
¼ pint (150 ml) dry white wine
2–2½ pints (1.2–1.5 l) cold water
1 small sliced onion
6–8 parsley stalks
1 slice lemon
½ bayleaf
1 small sprig thyme
4–6 peppercorns
¼–½ teaspoon salt

Sauce
the prawn butter
4 oz (100 g) plain flour
1 pint (600 ml) of the prawn fumet
1 pint (600 ml) milk
1 teaspoon (approx) tomato purée
¼ pint (150 ml) cream
squeeze lemon juice
salt and pepper

Puff Pastry Shapes
1 lb (450 g) ready made (Saxby or Jus-Roll) puff pastry
egg wash

Puff pastry shapes can be made several days ahead then kept in an airtight tin, ready to re-heat.

Briefly fry the prawn shells in butter

The shells and butter are poured into a piece of muslin

The muslin is squeezed and twisted to expel the butter

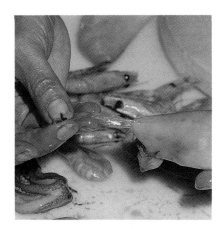

Removing the mouth which is in the centre of the squid

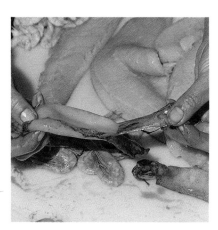

Skinning the squid

Withdrawing the transparent quill from the squid's body

Start by making the prawn butter and fish fumet. Then prepare and cook all the fish. Now make the sauce and combine it with the fish. The finished dish can be left for 24 hours ready to re-heat if the fish was really fresh.

Prawn Butter. Shell the prawns, and setting the prawns aside, heat the butter in a frying pan. Throw in the prawn shells and toss over the heat for 3–4 minutes.

Use the double-bladed knife. Scrape the prawn shells and butter into the Magimix bowl and process until finely chopped. Then turn the mixture into a large piece of muslin (or a clean tea towel or scrap of thin material) set over a bowl. Twist and squeeze the mixture to expel all the butter. It's amazing how much flavour you get from prawn shells which are normally thrown away!

Prawn Fumet. Wash the fish bones and skins, ideally removing the gills. Place the prawn shell residue into a pan and cover it with the fish bones and skins. Add all the remaining ingredients, tucking the herbs and peppercorns under the fish bones so they don't get skimmed off when you remove the froth. Bring to the boil, skim and simmer for 30–40 minutes (no longer or you can get a bitter taste from the bones). Strain through your rinsed muslin and use for cooking the fish and for the sauce. You can boil it down to intensify the flavour if you so wish.

The Fish. Skin all the fish, so much easier done with a sharp, flexible knife before the fish is cooked. Add the white fish skins to the fumet. Remove any bones you can; again this is so much easier before it is all cooked and hot.

Place the smoked haddock in a roomy saucepan and cover with cold water. Bring to the boil and set aside on the edge of the stove for about 10 minutes by which time it should be cooked. Drain off the water, pick out any bones, flake the fish into large chunks and set aside.

Wash the squid and remove the transparent beak-like mouth in the middle of the rosette of arms. Then pull the squid apart and discard the eyes and entrails. Pull out the transparent quill from the body. Cut body into rings and the legs into pieces. Poach for 3–4 minutes only in the hot prawn fumet, then drain and set aside.

Poach the white fish fillet in the hot prawn fumet until just cooked. Flake into large chunks and set aside.

Wash and clean the mussels, pull out the beards and discard any which will not close. Place in a roomy saucepan and toss, covered, over high heat for several minutes until the shells open. Remove the mussels and set aside. Discard the shells and strain the cooking liquid carefully into the fish fumet, using muslin to catch the sand.

Remove the black intestine from the scollops, if it's still there, and the hard muscle. Cut each into 3–4 pieces, the orange tongues into 2–3 pieces, and poach for several minutes until just firmed in a little of the prawn fumet. Drain and set aside. Hard boil the eggs if used.

Sauce. Strain the prawn fumet again through double muslin for it will be quite cloudy from cooking the fish.

Place the prawn butter, minus any watery residue, in a large saucepan. Add the flour and cook over gentle heat for 5–6 minutes; draw off the heat and wait for the sizzling to cease before adding measured prawn fumet and milk. Bring to the boil, whisking hard, and simmer very gently for 5–10 minutes. Season and add just enough tomato purée (this depends on how pink the prawns were) to make the sauce an attractive pinky colour. Add the cream, season and sharpen with a squeeze of lemon juice. Fold in all the seafood and roughly sliced, hard boiled eggs, if used.

If you are using it within several hours, keep it warm on the back of the stove to allow all the flavours to blend and mature. Then turn into a wide gratin dish and serve scattered with Puff Pastry Shapes and decorated with parsley.

To serve later. Turn into a greased, wide gratin dish, cover and cool. Re-heat, well covered, in a moderately hot oven (375°F/190°C/Gas 5) for about ¾–1 hour, stirring once or twice.

Puff Pastry Shapes. Roll the pastry to about ⅜ in. (9 mm) thickness. Either cut out letters with a very sharp knife (use a paper pattern for the letters or they will all come out different sizes!) and allow for the pastry to shrink in the cooking. Or cut into shapes – circles, diamonds, crescents or what you will, using a cutter.

Turn upside down onto a greased, damp baking sheet and bake in a hot oven (425°F/220°C/Gas 7) for about 10 minutes until well risen and brown. Then brush the tops with egg wash and continue to bake in a moderately hot oven (375°F/190°C/Gas 5) until really cooked and crisped right through; cover or lower the temperature if they are getting too brown. Re-warm in a slow oven before serving on top of the fish.

Braised Carrot with Cumin

I like to cut full sized carrots into strips with the french fry disc, then braise them gently in the oven in a little butter, flavoured with garlic and cumin. They are very easy to cook, all their goodness is conserved and they will keep warm quite happily.

10–12 people
5–6 lb (2.25–2.7 kg) large carrots
2½ oz (65 g) butter
1–2 cloves garlic
½–¾ teaspoon cumin seeds
¼ chicken stock cube (Knorr)
1 tablespoon sugar
plenty of fresh chopped parsley, chervil or fennel
salt and pepper

Use the french fry disc. Peel the carrots and cut into lengths which will fit sideways down the feed tube. Chip them, using firm pressure on the plunger. Heat the butter in a wide casserole, chop the garlic finely and add with the cumin, pounded up in a mortar. Fry until the garlic softens but do not let it brown. Now add the carrots, sugar and seasoning and toss around in the butter until glistening all over. Add the chicken stock cube to the juices in the bottom of the casserole, stir and cover closely with a butter paper pressed onto the carrots or with a piece of foil or bakewell paper between lid and casserole. Cook in a slow oven (300°F/150°C/Gas 2) for ¾–1¼ hours or until tender. Remove the lid and cook over a high heat to evaporate any excess moisture; check the seasoning and keep warm until ready to serve. Serve sprinkled heavily with fresh chopped parsley, chervil or fennel.

The squid is poached in the Prawn Fumet

Cutting out pretty shapes from the thinly rolled puff pastry

Wicked Chocolate Pudding

Wickedly rich, but who does not enjoy a slice of melting chocolate extravagance from time to time? This superb creation is based on a classic chocolate marquise from a great french chef, but by using the Magimix, it can be put together in moments rather than hours. I never can decide if I like it better plain or with the sponge fingers which certainly cut some of the richness. But either way, the coffee sauce just completes it.

10–12 people
5 oz (125 g) best dark chocolate (such as Menier)
5 egg yolks
8 oz (225 g) castor sugar
8 oz (225 g) very soft, lightly salted butter
5 oz (125 g) sifted cocoa powder
5 tablespoons hot water
12 fl oz (350 ml) chilled whipping cream
2 boxes sponge fingers } optional
6 fl oz (175 ml) strong black coffee } optional

A spot of butter keeps the sponge fingers in place

The soft and smooth chocolate mixture

The finished mixture being carefully poured into the prepared mould

Trimming sponge fingers level with chocolate

Checking that the mould is centrally placed on the serving dish before turning it over

The paper is carefully peeled off

Beautiful and decorative puddings really add something to a buffet table

Sauce

12 fl oz (350 ml) whipping cream
vanilla sugar to taste
1½ teaspoons powdered coffee

Line an oblong mould of approximately 12 × 4 in. (30 × 10 cm) with bakewell paper (or oiled greaseproof paper) and, if using sponge fingers dip them briefly in black coffee before lining the mould with them, (a spot of butter will help to hold the sponge fingers in place). You can dispense with the sponge fingers altogether and just pour the chocolate mixture into the bakewell lined mould but this makes a very rich pudding.

Place the broken chocolate in a bowl over hot water and leave to become completely soft. Ensure the butter is absolutely soft but not runny. Now gather together all your ingredients because, once you start, you want to work quickly without a pause.

First whip the chilled cream in a cold bowl with a balloon whisk until it is holding soft peaks.

Use the double-bladed knife. Place the egg yolks and sugar in the bowl and beat until pale. Add in the melted chocolate and, bit by bit, the soft butter (but not while the chocolate is too warm or the butter could oil) and finally the cocoa powder and hot water alternately. You should now have a very soft, smooth mixture. Add the chocolate mixture to the whipped cream (the chocolate cold but still runny) and whisk together with a balloon whisk until completely amalgamated. Pour into the prepared mould and leave to set in the fridge.

Sauce. Mix the powdered coffee and sugar with 1 tablespoon boiling water, stir until dissolved and mix with the cream. Serve in a jug.

To Serve. Turn the pudding out and, if you wish, decorate with piped whipped cream and grated or flaked chocolate.

Vegetables in Sweet-Sour Ginger Dressing

Perhaps you can tell from this recipe that I have recently come back from a culinary trip to the Orient and that my twenty year love of chinese food has been endorsed and expanded. For this I wanted an attractive salad of vegetables, dressed with an exciting and tasty dressing; easy to prepare, easy to serve and easy to eat for a buffet party.

I started by preparing classic Chiang Ts'u (ginger slivers in vinegar) and varied it by adding more sugar to make a sweet-sour taste and a little cinnamon and coriander for flavour. I am delighted with the result. I find the dressing is very attractive and appeals to most people and it can be used with various vegetable and fruit combinations.

10–12 people
Sweet-Sour Ginger Dressing
6–8 thin slices (about the size of a 10p piece)
    fresh root ginger
3 tablespoons sugar
6 tablespoons wine vinegar
1 tabespoon coriander seeds
1½ in.–2 in. (5 cm) stick cinnamon
12–18 tablespoons light oil (sunflower, groundnut, etc)
salt and pepper

Version 1. Courgette, Mushroom and Prawn
2½ lb (1.15 kg) baby courgettes
1 lb (450 g) firm button mushrooms
8–10 oz (225–275 g) best quality prawns

Version 2. Mixed Fruit and Vegetables
1½ lb (675 g) tomatoes
1–2 cucumber
½–1 lb (225–450 g) black or green grapes
3–4 pears
1 pineapple or melon
some prawns (optional)

Sweet-Sour Ginger Dressing. Pound the coriander in a mortar; place in a saucepan with the stick of cinnamon and vinegar and heat.

Cut the slices of ginger into narrow slivers and put in a bowl with the sugar. Pour over the hot vinegar, coriander and cinnamon and leave until cold. Remove the cinnamon. Season with salt and pepper and whisk in the oil.

Courgettes, Mushroom and Prawn. *Use the 4 mm slicing disc.* Top and tail the courgettes, stack them carefully upright in the feed tube and slice. Bring a large pan of water to the boil and salt heavily (about 1 tablespoon to each 2 pints (1.2 l) water; this keeps the courgettes green and is washed off when they are refreshed). Throw in the courgettes and boil for ½ minute only; drain at once and refresh under the cold tap (do this in several batches for large numbers). Drain well, press out all moisture in a kitchen cloth or on kitchen paper and then add them to the dressing (this can be done up to 4 hours ahead). Half an hour or so before serving rinse and dry the mushrooms, cut into halves or quarters and toss into the dressing with the prawns (reserving a few to decorate the dish). Toss well and turn into a serving dish, scattering the reserved prawns on top. Serve fairly soon or the mushrooms will discolour and go flabby.

Mixed Fruit and Vegetables. *Use the 4 mm slicing disc.* Slice the cucumber, lay in a colander, sprinkle with salt and press with a plate and weight for ½ hour. Squeeze well to expel liquid and add cucumber to the dressing.

Prepare all the fruit and vegetables and add to the dressing as you do them. Peel and quarter the tomatoes, squeezing out most of the juice and pips; peel, quarter, core and cut the pears into segments; peel, core, slice and cut the pineapple into segments; halve the melon, remove seeds and scoop into balls; finally, halve and de-seed the grapes. Toss the mixture well together and turn into a serving bowl. Serve well chilled, scattered with prawns if you wish.

———— : ————

Turkey with Tarragon Mousseline Sauce

Poach the turkey inside a meat roasting bag with flavouring vegetables, herbs and just a little liquid. The whole bag is set in a large pan of boiling water, so we get all the benefits of poaching but also end up with a small quantity of superbly flavoured liquid for our sauce. The finished cubed turkey, in its delicately flavoured sauce is easy to eat, not likely to spill and is a welcome change from the cold chicken in sauce one is so often offered. The preparations can all be done 1–2 days ahead and are really very simple.

The turkey, vegetables, herbs, wine and stock are all contained in a roaster bag which is then poached in boiling water

If you cannot get fresh, you can make this with the best flavoured dried tarragon, adding some fresh chives or parsley for colour.

10–12 people
10 lb (4.5 kg) fresh or frozen turkey
1 large roaster or boil-in bag
2 onions
2 carrots
2 sticks celery
2 slices lemon from a thin-skinned lemon
bouquet garni made up of 2 tablespoons dried
    tarragon, 1 bayleaf, 4–5 parsley stalks, 2–3 sprigs
    thyme, 6 peppercorns and 2 cloves
¼–½ pint (150–300 ml) dry white wine
1 pint (600 ml) light chicken stock or water and
    chicken stock cube
salt and pepper

Tarragon Mousseline Sauce

1 egg and 2 yolks
2–3 tablespoons lemon juice
¾ pint (450 ml) mixed olive and light oil
handful of fresh or 1½ tablespoons dried tarragon
1 tablespoons dijon mustard
½ pint (300 ml) reduced turkey stock
½ pint (300 ml) whipping cream
grated rinds of 2–3 lemons
salt and pepper

If using a frozen turkey, give it a good 36–48 hours, or even longer in a cold larder, to thaw thoroughly.

Remove any bag of giblets from the crop end. Season the bird inside and out and place the bouquet garni, done up in muslin, inside it. Place the turkey, with the neck and giblets minus the liver, in the roaster bag with the roughly cut-up onions, carrots, celery, lemon slices, wine and stock. Seal up tightly. Place the turkey in its bag on a trivet (or anything to keep it off the bottom of the pan and even a couple of crossed wooden spoons will do) in a large pan and add boiling water to cover it. It will tend to float but to keep it down, I use an inverted saucepan lid which, once the lid of the pan is on, keeps the turkey submerged.

If you have not got a large enough pan in which to poach the turkey, you will have to cook it, inside its roaster bag, in a large casserole or meat roasting pan in the oven, just setting as much boiling water around it as you can and making sure the roaster bag is well ballooned so the turkey is cooking in as much steamy moisture as possible.

Bring the water back to the boil, then maintain a very slow simmer for 1½ hours. Take the pan off the stove and leave the turkey to cool in the liquid.

Pour off the water and remove the bag of turkey, taking care not to let the bag burst therefore losing the precious liquid. Open the bag and drain off the stock; (if it's already set to jelly, warm it) then pass it through a double layer of muslin so it is really clear. Boil fast to reduce it to about ½ pint (300 ml), cool again, and it should now be very strongly flavoured. Take the turkey meat off the bones, cut into generous chunks and season lightly; this should give you about 3½–4 lb (1.6–1.8 kg) of meat. Set aside, well covered, until ready to fold into the sauce.

Tarragon Mousseline Sauce. *Use the double-bladed knife.* Place the egg and yolks in the Magimix bowl with the mustard, very light seasoning, the tarragon leaves pulled from the stalks or dried tarragon, 1 tablespoon lemon juice and some of the grated lemon rind. Process for 10–20 seconds then gradually, in a fine thread, add the oil to make a mayonnaise; when the mixture takes and starts to slurp around the bowl, add the oil a little faster in a steady stream. Once all the oil is in and you have a nice thick mayonnaise, add the reduced and cold turkey stock, correct the seasoning, lemon rind and juice and tarragon, remembering that the cream will soften the flavour. Turn into a large bowl (big enough to hold all the diced turkey and sauce) then whip the cream lightly until it is softly holding its shape and fold it into the sauce. Correct the flavour and seasoning again and fold in the turkey meat. Taste again, then cover closely and chill until ready to serve (up to 24 hours is fine).

To Serve. Mound on a large meat plate or attractive serving dish, surround with a generous necklace of watercress and decorate with fresh tarragon leaves or scissored chives if you have no tarragon.

——————— : ———————

Red Pepper and Green Bean Salad

This most attractively coloured salad is just right with the creamy tarragon turkey. By blanching the red peppers as well as the beans, one softens their quite powerful flavour but does not lose their crisp texture. The shallot dressing, preferably with its hint of hazelnut or walnut oil, seems just right for this salad.

10–12 people
4–5 red peppers
1½ lb (675 g) baby french beans

Shallot Dressing
1 teaspoon dijon mustard
2 shallots or a slice of onion
3 tablespoons wine vinegar
4 tablespoons hazelnut or walnut oil or use all
    olive oil
5 tablespoons light oil
½ teaspoon salt
⅛ teaspoon pepper

Top and tail the beans and break into 2 in. (5 cm) lengths. Blanch by tossing the beans into plenty of heavily salted water (lots of salt keeps the beans bright green and washes off when you refresh them later) and boil until they are cooked but still very crisp (4–8 minutes approx). Drain, refresh under the cold tap to set the colour and remove excess salt and drain again.

Use the 4 mm slicing disc. Cut the peppers in half lengthways, remove the seeds and stalk, and fit the halves one inside another before packing them into the feed tube and slicing. Blanch the peppers for 1 minute only in plenty of boiling, heavily salted water; then drain in a colander and refresh under the cold tap to arrest the cooking and set the colour;

drain well. Combine with the beans and toss in the dressing. This salad is better dressed an hour or so before serving.

Shallot Dressing. *Use the double-bladed knife.* Place the roughly cut up shallots or onion in the Magimix bowl with the salt, pepper, mustard and vinegar. Process to chop the shallot finely and dissolve the salt, pouring the oils in down the feed tube to make a nice thick dressing. Use to dress the beans and peppers.

——————— : ———————

Fresh Pineapple Tart

This pâte sucrée pastry case has a layer of rum flavoured, cream cheese filling and is topped by rounds of glazed, poached pineapple. It makes a super pudding for all sorts of occasions. You can vary it by changing the flavouring of the cream to vanilla, lemon or kirsch and using whatever fruit are in season such as kiwis, strawberries or peaches.

for 6–8 people
Pâte Sucrée
8 oz (225 g) plain flour
5½ oz (155 g) soft butter
2 oz (50 g) icing sugar
1 egg yolk
1–2 tablespoons cold water
a few drops vanilla essence (optional)
pinch of salt

Cream Cheese Filling
2 oz (50 g) soft butter
2 oz (50 g) vanilla sugar
1 egg yolk
8 oz (225 g) unsalted cream cheese (Eden Vale
    Somerset soft cream cheese etc.)
2 teaspoons rum
1 lemon

Pineapple
2 medium or 1 large ripe pineapple
6 oz (175 g) granulated sugar
4 fl oz (100 ml) water
2–3 tablespoons rum

Glaze
6–8 tablespoons apricot jam
1–2 tablespoons rum

It is easier to peel the whole pineapple before slicing and coring it

The pastry case is balanced on a tin so that the outside of the flan tin can be removed without damaging the pastry

The yellow pineapple slices look very decorative when arranged on the cream cheese filling

To choose a ripe pineapple, look for one that is not too hard, has a faint aroma and whose centre leaves will pluck out quite easily. The autumn pineapples are from the Cape, arrive by sea, and having ripened on the way they are usually almost ready to eat. By December, the Caribbean fruit are arriving by air; these take much longer to ripen, often as much as a week or so. So think ahead or go to a quality fruit shop which sells them ripe.

Pâte Sucrée. *Use the double-bladed knife.* Place the soft butter and the sugar in the Magimix with the salt, egg yolk, water and vanilla, if used. Process for just long enough to mix thoroughly. Sift in the flour and process until just incorporated, stopping to stir down once. Turn out onto a floured board and form into a flat disc; it will be rather sticky at this stage so slip into a plastic bag and chill for about 2 hours.

Roll the pastry to fit a 11 in. (28 cm) flan tin, press into the corners well and roll off the excess; prick the base, line with tinfoil and baking beans and bake blind in a hot oven (400°F/200°C/Gas 6) for 7–10 minutes. Once the pastry has set, remove the tinfoil and beans and continue to bake in a moderately hot oven (375°F/190°C/Gas 5) until it is a pale golden brown and cooked through; tiny bubbles will now show on the pastry which denote that the flour is fully cooked and the lovely buttery flavour will be apparent to the taste. Cool on a rack.

Cream Cheese Filling. *Use the double-bladed knife.* Place the soft butter and sugar in the Magimix and process until well creamed. Then add the egg yolk, cream cheese (not too cold from the fridge or it can be a bit firm for spreading), the rum, a grating of lemon rind and a good squeeze of juice. Process together until well mixed, but not for more than about 20 seconds or the cream cheese may curdle and go buttery. If necessary, thin with a drop of milk to spreading consistency. Spread the filling over the base of the cold, cooked pastry shell and arrange the pineapple slices on it. Spoon over the glaze and leave to set.

Pineapple. Dissolve the sugar in the water and simmer for several minutes before adding the rum. Peel, slice and core the pineapple; poach the slices in the syrup for about 5 minutes then drain in a sieve. When cold, pat dry on kitchen paper and arrange on the cream cheese filling.

Glaze. Sieve the apricot jam and stir in the rum and 1–2 tablespoons of the poaching syrup. Spoon over the pineapple slices to glaze.

Index

Figures in bold type indicate recipes
Figures in italics indicate photographs